Greater Chicago Historical Tour Guide

By D. Ray Wilson

A Roads Book

COVER PHOTO: *One of the many dinosaur exhibits displayed at the Field Museum of Natural History in Chicago. A favorite of the visitors to the museum, this great hall is filled with fossil remains and skeletons of prehistoric mammals, reptiles, birds and fishes. The exhibit space is dominated by skeletal reconstructions of the Mastodon, Mammoth, and a 72-foot long Apatosaurus. The dinosaur exhibit hall is located on the museum's second floor.*

Other Books in this Series by D. Ray Wilson
"Wyoming Historical Tour Guide"
"Iowa Historical Tour Guide"
"Kansas Historical Tour Guide"
"Nebraska Historical Tour Guide"
"Missouri Historical Tour Guide"

ABOUT THE AUTHOR—D. Ray Wilson, born and raised in California, has been a newspaper man all of his adult life, serving on newspapers in Nebraska, Kansas, California, Arizona, and Illinois. He is author of *"The Folks," "Fort Kearny on the Platte,"* and *"Episode on Hill 616"* in addition to his series of historical tour guides. Wilson, who received his journalism degree from Northern Illinois University, is publisher and editor of two Illinois daily newspapers and several weeklies. In 1985, he received an honorary Doctor of Letters degree from Judson College, Elgin, Illinois. He is listed in several editions of "Who's Who" and is founder and Chairman of the Board of the DuPage Heritage Gallery, Wheaton, Illinois.

Dedicated to my daughters
Jeri Rae, Vicky Joy, Julianne, Margaret Erin

Author: D. Ray Wilson
GREATER CHICAGO HISTORICAL TOUR GUIDE

1st Edition, 1989

Published by Crossroads Communications
Carpentersville, Illinois, 60110-0007
Manufactured in the United States of America

Library of Congress Catalog Number: 89-60056
International Standard Book Number: 0-916445-24-0

Copyright 1989 by Crossroads Communications. All rights reserved. No part of this book may used or reproduced in any manner whatsoever without written permission of the publisher except in the case of brief quotations in articles and reviews. For information write: Crossroads Communications, P.O. Box 7, Carpentersville, IL. 60110-0007.

The present Great Seal of Illinois was authorized by the General Assembly on March 7, 1867, but was not used until 1868. When Illinois Territory was created in 1809 the seal (upper left) was designed and first used on February 4, 1810. The first Great Seal (upper right) was adopted after statehood and used until about 1839. The second Great Seal (lower left) was used until October 24, 1868. The present Great Seal (lower right) was first used on October 26, 1868. Secretary of State Sharon Tyndale brought about the creation of the seal which exists today.

GREATER CHICAGO

Includes the county seats and counties of Cook, Lake, McHenry, Kane, DuPage and Will.

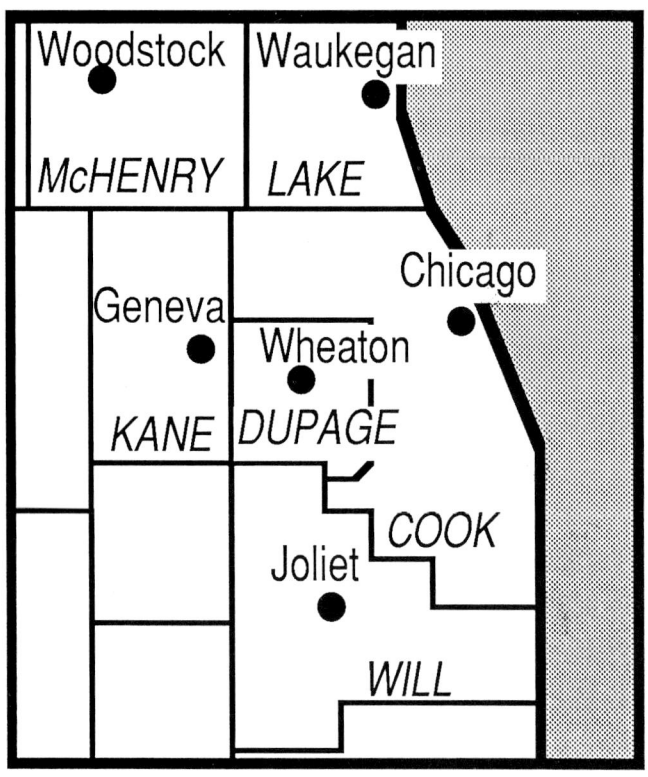

Table of Contents

INTRODUCTION 1

CHAPTER 1 5
Formation of Chicago

CHAPTER 2 9
Layout of the City

CHAPTER 3 19
Chicago—An Overview

CHAPTER 4 53
The Gangster Era

CHAPTER 5 65
Chicago Museums and Historical Sites

CHAPTER 6 101
Elsewhere in Cook County

CHAPTER 7 129
Touring DuPage County

CHAPTER 8 157
Touring Lake County

CHAPTER 9 175
Touring McHenry County

CHAPTER 10 187
Touring Kane County

CHAPTER 11 211
Touring Will County

CHAPTER 12 221
Miscellaneous

INDEX 239

Introduction

This book is written for those persons interested in history, particularly American history. It is not a comprehensive work but is meant to serve as a reference book for those persons touring the Greater Chicago area. Area residents may find it helpful in learning more about their communities or the area generally. It should be a helpful guide to the area museums and historical attractions for those out-of-area visitors.

The Greater Chicago area includes Cook, DuPage, Lake, McHenry, Kane and Will counties. We have located the museums and historic sites in each county as well as those in Chicago.

Many of the photos appearing in this tour guide have been taken by the author and others furnished by various individuals and organizations. The information regarding museum hours was correct and accurate as of February 15, 1989.

This work began in 1985 and our research came from books, newspaper articles and features, and copies of publications and pamphlets provided by local historical societies and chambers of commerce.

We have spent 20 years in the area and have visited all of the communities covered as well as most of the museums and other attractions. It is an interesting area, steeped in history.

Among the most famous and most popular attractions surely must be the Field Museum of Natural History, the Shedd Aquarium, Adler Planetarium, Museum of Science and Industry, and the Art Institute of Chicago. There are several others that are noteworthy in their own right. The local history museums aid visitors in gaining a better understanding of the rigors of the early-day immigrants and settlers and those who followed.

The personalities connected with the area are diverse. Famous writers, such as Ernest Hemingway, Ray Bradbury, John Dos Passos, Carl Sandburg, Harriet Monroe, and Gwendolyn Brooks; architects Frank Lloyd Wright, George Maher, and Louis Sullivan; sports greats Harold "Red" Grange, Amos Alonzo Stagg,

Charles Comiskey, and Johnny Weissmuller; entertainers with such names as Jack Benny, Edgar Bergen, Gloria Swanson and Robert Ryan; scientists Dr. Enrico Fermi, Edwin Powell Hubble, and Grote Reber; and the great entrepreneurs Marshall Field, Potter Palmer, George M. Pullman, and Cyrus McCormick had their roots here. The most notorious gangsters, Al Capone, Bugs Moran, John Dillinger, and "Baby Face" Nelson, also are part of the area's history.

Frances Willard became famous as a leader of the Women's Christian Temperance Union. Jane Addams and Ellen Gates Starr founded Hull House, Chicago's first settlement house for immigrants.

The Elgin National Road Races drew the top racing drivers in the country, Barney Oldfield, Ray Harroun, Eddie Rickenbacher, and Ralph DePalma, for a decade starting in 1911.

Many celebrities have had a connection with DuPage County —Judge Elbert Gary, who organized US Steel; John "Bet-A-Million" Gates, founder of the Texaco Oil Company; Reverend Billy Graham, internationally known evangelist; Everett Mitchell, an early radio pioneer; Dr. Kenneth Taylor, who converted 66 books of the Bible into modern style and language; and others.

There are modern-day heroes as well. Astronaut Eugene Cernan, who with Harrison Schmitt, was the the last man on the moon. He was born in Chicago and raised in the suburbs. Walter Payton gained fame as the great running back for the Chicago Bears. Sherrill Milnes, from Downers Grove, has gained worldwide acclaim as a Verdi baritone with the Metopolitan Opera.

Abraham Lincoln gained the nomination for the presidency at the first Republican convention—held in Chicago. Several other national conventions have been held here over the years.

Native Elmer E. Ellsworth was one of the first heroes of the Civil War. There have been many Congressional Medal of Honor recipients from this area and they are listed.

There have been a number of tragedies recorded in the area; fires and riots have taken heavy tolls as have several ship accidents.

The Great Fire of 1871 left over 100,000 persons homeless, took several hundred lives, and could have been the end of Chicago. Instead, the city bounced back and within five years was one of America's most vibrant, emerging metropolises.

One police officer was killed, six fatally wounded and 68 others injured in The Haymarket Square Riot of 1886. A rioter was killed and a dozen others wounded. Four of the rioters were hanged and two were given life sentences for the bombing.

Literally hundreds of persons have had some involvement in the preparation of this book. Not only did they provide information and other material but assisted in the proofreading as our manuscript was being prepared for print.

While it is impossible to list everyone who has lent a hand, I do want to acknowledge the contributions made by two persons — Beatrice J. Wilson, my wife, who has offered encouragement and has accompanied me on some of my trips exploring the region, and Alice McCoy, who helped with a myriad of details in the actual production of book.

Special thanks to John Whyte, Director, Community Services, *Joliet Herald-News* for his help in providing information and photos for Will County. We also acknowledge the assistance of the staff at the *Elgin Daily Courier-News* and D.J. Schumacher, Editor, *Waukegan News Sun*.

We are grateful to the museum curators and directors who provided us with information. They also assisted in the proofreading, particularly their own listings.

Many of the chambers of commerce also assisted in providing us with information about their communities. The Chicago Convention and Visitors Bureau was most helpful, especially in providing some of the photos which are credited.

We recommend that visitors obtain a good map of the area. Visitors and tourists will find chambers of commerce most helpful. Additional information may be obtained by contacting the offices listed here:

Illinois Office of Tourism, State of Illinos Center, 100 W. Randolph St., Chicago 60601 or phone 917-4732.

Illinois Tourist Information Center, 310 S. Michigan Ave., Chicago 60604 or phone 793-2094.

Aurora Area Convention and Tourism Council, 40 W. Downer Pl., Aurora 60506 or phone 897-5581.

Chicago Convention and Visitors Bureau, McCormick Place on the Lake, Chicago 60616 or phone 567-8500.

Chicago/South Convention and Visitors Bureau, 900 Ridge Rd., Homewood 60430 or phone 798-7093.

Chicago Tourism Council, Historic Water Tower in the Park, 806 N. Michigan Ave., Chicago 60611 or phone 280-5740.

Elgin Area Convention and Visitors Bureau, 24 E. Chicago St., Elgin 60120 or phone 741-5660.

Greater Woodfield Convention and Visitors Bureau, 1375 E. Woodfield Rd., Schaumburg 60173. Inside Illinois phone 1-800-624-8326. Outside Illinois phone 1-800-847-4849.

Heritage Corridor Convention and Visitors Bureau, 81 N. Chicago St., Joliet 60431 or phone 815-727-2323.

Lake County Convention and Visitors Bureau, 414 N. Sheridan Rd., Waukegan 60085. Inside Illinois phone 1-800-847-4864. Outside Illinois phone 1-800-525-3669.

Naperville Area Chamber of Commerce, 9 W. Jackson, Naperville 60566 or phone 355-4141.

Rosemont/O'Hare Convention Bureau, 9291 W. Bryn Mawr Ave., Rosemont 60018 or phone 823-2100.

St. Charles Convention and Visitors Bureau, 201 N. 1st Ave., St. Charles 60174 or phone 377-6161.

We hope you enjoy the Greater Chicago area and its offerings.

D. Ray Wilson
Sleepy Hollow, IL

February, 1989

Chapter 1
Formation of Chicago

This chapter covers Greater Chicago made up of Cook, DuPage, Kane, Lake, McHenry, and Will Counties

This chapter provides a brief history on how and when the counties where organized. Also listed are the colleges and universities in this six county area.

Chapter 1
Formation of Greater Chicago

Greater Chicago covered in this work includes Cook, DuPage, Kane, Lake, McHenry, and Will counties.

Cook county was established January 15, 1831 with Chicago selected as the county seat. It was named for **Daniel P. Cook**, pioneer lawyer, first Attorney General of Illinois, and member of Congress from 1819 to 1827. Originally the county boundaries included today's DuPage, McHenry and Will counties. Today, it encompasses 954 square miles.

The University of Illinois has two branches located in Chicago—Chicago Circle and the Medical Center. Chicago State University, 95th St. and Martin Luther King Dr., is the oldest public university in the Chicago area, founded as Teacher Training School, Blue Island, in 1869. It became the Cook County Normal School in 1869. Northeastern Illinois University, 5500 N. St. Louis Ave., opened its doors in 1961.

Other Cook county colleges and universities include School of the Art Institute of Chicago (1866); Columbia College, Chicago (1944); Concordia Teachers College, River Forest (1864); DePaul University, Chicago (1898); Illinois College of Optometry, Chicago (1947); Illinois Institute of Technology, Chicago (1892); Loyola University of Chicago (1870); Mallinckrodt College of the North Shore, Wilmette (1918); Mundelein College, Chicago (1930); North Park College, Chicago (1891); Roosevelt University, Chicago (1945); Rosary College, River Forest (1848); St. Xavier College, Chicago (1846); Spertus College of Judaica, Chicago (1927); and Vandercook College of Music, Chicago (1909).

Wheaton is the county seat of DuPage county, established February 18, 1839. It covers 331 square miles. The county was named for the DuPage River. Wheaton is the home of Wheaton College, founded in 1860. Other colleges in DuPage county are Bethany Theological Seminary, Oak Brook (1911); Elmhurst College, Naperville (1861); and Northern Baptist Theological Seminary, Lombard (1913). The Illinois Youth Center-DuPage is located at Warrenville and is a facility for female juvenile offenders.

Covering 515 square miles, Kane county was formed January 16, 1836. The county was named for **Senator Elias K. Kane**, first Secretary of State of Illinois. Geneva is the county seat. The two largest cities in Kane county are Aurora and Elgin. Aurora is home of Aurora College (1893) and Elgin is home of Judson College (1963). Illinois Youth Centers, correctional facilities for male juveniles, are located at St. Charles and Valley View in the county. The St. Charles facility was opened in 1901.

Lake county, named for Lake Michigan, was formed March 1, 1839 with Waukegan as the county seat. It covers 457 square miles. The colleges and universities in Lake county are Barat College, Lake Forest (1919); Lake Forest College, Lake Forest (1857); National College of Education, Evanston (1886); Northwestern University, Evanston (1851); and Trinity College, Deerfield (1952).

Woodstock is the county seat of McHenry county, established January 16, 1836. The county covers 611 square miles. It was named in honor of **Gen. William McHenry**, a veteran of the War of 1812 and the Black Hawk War. The largest communities are Crystal Lake and McHenry.

Will county, named for **Conrad Will**, member of the Constitutional Convention of 1818 and a member of the first to ninth General Assemblies, was established, January 12, 1836, with Joliet as the county seat. Will county covers 845 square miles. Governors State University, University Park, was established in 1969. Other colleges and universities in Will county are Lewis University, Lockport (1950), and College of St. Francis, Joliet (1930). The Joliet Correctional Center, the state's oldest correctional facility, dates back to 1858. Stateville, the state's largest correctional facility, was completed in 1919. The Illinois Youth Center-Joliet handles more aggressive and older juvenile offenders.

Chapter 2
Layout of the City

Highlights on the Chicago sports scene—a list of some of the great sports events and super stars who have appeared in Chicago down through the years.

Chapter 2
Layout of the City

Chicago is divided into four sections. These include Downtown Chicago, the North Side, the West Side, and the South Side.

The main downtown area extends about 10 blocks south of the Chicago River. The river's south branch borders it on the west; the lake on the east. Within this area, elevated trains run along a rectangular "loop" of tracks five blocks wide and seven blocks long to give this area the nickname, the Loop. The trains travel between the Loop and suburbs at the edge of city. The financial district is located on LaSalle St. The Midwest Stock Exchange and the Chicago Board of Trade are located here. Fourteen blocks of Michigan Ave., north of the Chicago River, make up the city's "Magnificent Mile," home of elegant stores, restaurants, hotels and office buildings. One of the world's largest commercial buildings, the Merchandise Mart, is just across the river from Wacker Dr. Soldier Field, on the lakefront south of Grant Park, is home of the Chicago Bears of the National Football League.

The North Side, stretching from downtown to about nine miles north and 13 miles northwest, is almost entirely residential. It is here one finds the Gold Coast and Old Town. Lincoln Park, the city's largest and most popular park begins north of the Gold Coast. Southwest of Old Town is the depressed and crime-ridden Cabrini-Green Housing Project. The rest of the North Side consists of middle-class neighborhoods. The Chicago Cubs of the National League play baseball in Wrigley Field on the North Side.

The West Side, lying west of the Loop between Grand Ave. on the north and the Chicago Sanitary and Ship Canal on the south, includes the industrial districts along the canal and residential neighborhoods further out. The Eisenhower Expressway cuts through the West Side between the Loop and the western suburbs. It cuts through the Chicago Post Office, the world's largest post office building. The Chicago Black Hawks of the National Hockey League and the Chicago Bulls of the National Basketball Association play in the Chicago Stadium on the West Side.

The South Side stretches 16 miles south of downtown and the West Side and covers more than half the city's area. Two well-known neighborhoods are Chinatown and Bridgeport. Chinatown has a small residential section and a line of restaurants and gift

Arthur J. Goldberg, a native Chicagoan, has served as Secretary of Labor, a Supreme Court justice, and U. S. Ambassador to the United Nations. He was born in 1908.

shops. Bridgeport has been the home of four of Chicago's mayors. The famous Union Stock Yards, which closed in 1971, once supplied meat to most of the nation. The Chicago White Sox of the American League play baseball in Comiskey Park on the South Side.

Chicago has dominated American architecture since the late 1800s. Two of the important styles of architecture to emerge early were the Chicago school and prairie school. Those whose work produced the Chicago school were **William L. Jenney**, **Daniel H. Burnham** and **Louis Sullivan**. **Frank Lloyd Wright** developed the prairie school style. The glass-and-steel style, a second generation of the Chicago school, was introduced by the German architect **Ludwig Mies van der Rohe**.

Jenney designed the world's first skyscaper, the 10-story Home Insurance Building, in downtown. This and other Chicago school early buildings have been demolished.

Among some of the more prominent Chicagoans have been or are **Clarence Darrow** (1857-1938), famous criminal lawyer who defended **Eugene Debs** in an 1894 labor strike, Loeb and Leopold in their 1924 trial for the murder of Bobby Franks, and defended the right to teach evolution in Tennessee schools in the 1925 John T. Scopes case; **John Dos Passos** (1896-1970), noted novelist whose work was dominated by social and political themes; **Arthur J. Goldberg**, former U.S. Ambassador to the United Nations, Associate Justice of the Supreme Court, and Secretary of Labor in President Kennedy's Cabinet; **John Gunther** (1901-70), a journalist who gained fame for a series of books that drew on his observations as a foreign correspondent for the *Chicago Daily News*; and **Robert R. McCormick**, who, as publisher, made the *Chicago Tribune* one of the nation's most important newspapers.

On the Chicago Sports Scene

One of football's first superstars was **Harold "Red" Grange**, who gained fame as the University of Illinois' "Galloping Ghost" before joining the Chicago Bears in 1925. He and Bears' owner/coach George Halas are credited with the creation of the National Football League as we know it today. Probably one of Grange's most memorable games occurred at the University of Illinois the afternoon of October 18, 1924, when he scored four touchdowns in the first 12 minutes of play against undefeated University of Michigan. He scored a fifth touchdown in this game for the "Fighting Illini" to defeat Michigan. Grange was one of the 17 charter members inducted into the Pro Football Hall of Fame in Canton, Ohio, when it was dedicated, September 7, 1963.

Amos Alonzo Stagg (1862-1965), known as football's "Grand Old Man," was the oldest active coach in the country with the greatest number of coaching seasons to his credit. He coached at the University of Chicago for 41 years. When he retired at the age of 70 he went on to coach at College of Pacific for another 14 years and then to Susquehanna (PA) University from 1947 to 1952. He was 90 years old when he gave up his coaching career of over 60 years.

The great swimmer **Johnny Weissmuller** was a product of the Illinois Athletic Club. He won five gold medals in the 1924 and 1928 Olympics. Weissmuller broke many world swimming records before he retired from competition. Later he starred in several of the Tarzan films.

The famous "long count" boxing match between **Jack Dempsey** and **Gene Tunney** was held at Soldier Field, September 22, 1927. Dempsey was fighting to regain his world heavyweight title he had lost to Tunney a year earlier. In the seventh round, Dempsey knocked Tunney down but the referee, **Dave Barry**, refused to begin the count for five seconds because Dempsey had not gone to a neutral corner. Tunney got up at the count of nine and went on to win the fight on points.

Heavyweight boxer **Joe Louis** began his professional career in Chicago in 1934. During his 17-year boxing career, Louis appeared in the ring in Chicago 19 times. He won the world heavyweight title in June, 1937, by knocking out **James J. Braddock**, and held it until his retirement in 1949. The "Brown Bomber" defended his title 25 times, scoring 20 knockouts.

Two other great boxing matches occurred in the 1930s.

June 23, 1933, **Barney Ross**, a West Sider, defeated **Tony Canzoneri** for the lightweight title. Four years later, Joe Louis knocked out James J. Braddock, the heavyweight champion, in the eighth round of a fight held at Comiskey Park. Braddock had defeated Max Baer for the title in 1935..

Perhaps one of the bloodiest boxing matches occurred, July 16, 1947, in Chicago Stadium. **Rocky Graziano** knocked out **Tony Zale** in the sixth round of a brutal and bloody middleweight championship bout. Zale had defeated Graziano a year earlier to retain his middleweight crown. A year after the 1947 fight, Zale regained his title by knocking Graziano out in the third round.

Chicago boasts two major league baseball teams—the White Sox, founded by **Charles Comiskey**, March 21, 1900, and the Cubs, founded by **William A. Hulbert**, in 1876, the same year the National League was founded.

The Chicago Black Hawks played their first National Hockey League game in 1926 at the Coliseum. They won their first Stanley Cup, April 10, 1934, when they defeated Detroit, 1 to 0.

The Chicago Bulls was founded, in 1966, as an expansion team in the National Basketball Association. Their 33 wins in the 1966-67 season remains as a record for an NBA expansion team.

The Great Walter Payton

Walter Payton, who retired in 1988 after 13 years with the Chicago Bears, is the National Football League's all-time leading rusher with 16,726 yards. Payton owns 10 NFL records and 25 Bears' records. His best season was 1977, his third, when he ran for 1,852 yards (a team record) and scored 14 touchdowns. He has scored more points (750) and has more touchdowns (125) than anyone in Bears' history. The 5-foot-11, 202-pound Payton, who lives in suburban Barrington, played in 190 regular-season games and started in 184. He also played and started in nine playoff games. He rushed for 61 yards in the Bears' 46-10 win over New England in Super Bowl XX, January 26, 1986, at New Orleans.

The Chicago Bear's great running back, Walter Payton, retired in 1988.

Harold "Red" Grange became a gridiron hero in the 1920s while playing for the University of Illinois and the Chicago Bears. He gained the sobriquet, "The Wheaton Iceman," early in his football career at the university. He worked every summer as an iceman in Wheaton as part of his individual physical conditioning for the football seasons. He won All-American honors and Grantland Rice, the noted sportswriter, first called him the "Galloping Ghost" following the October 18, 1924 game with Michigan when he scored four touchdowns in 12 minutes. He joined the Chicago Bears in the late fall of 1925 where he became an instant success as a running back. He made his pro debut in a game against the Chicago Cardinals in Wrigley Field, Thanksgiving day, 1925.

Red Grange was one of the 17 charter members inducted into the Pro Football Hall of Fame in Canton, Ohio, when it was dedicated September 7, 1963. Shown with Grange (wearing the sunglasses) is Jim Conzelman, a former pro player and coach.

Chapter 3
Chicago—An Overview

Highlights of some of the great and small historical events and happenings of a great city.

A brief review of Chicago's history...the personalities who helped the Windy City achieve greatness...and some of its scoundrels. Also covered are some of the tragedies that have befallen the city.

Chapter 3
Chicago—An Overview

Chicago (pop. 3,005,072), county seat of Cook County, was platted in 1830 and incorporated as a village in 1833; as a city in 1837.

Father Jacques Marquette and **Louis Joliet** arrived in 1673 during their exploration and expedition through the Mississippi Valley to the Gulf of Mexico. Next came **Henry Tonti**, a soldier of fortune and friend and associate of Robert Cavalier, Sieur de La Salle. Tonti arrived at the Chicago River in 1681 to outfit La Salle's expedition southward into the Mississippi Valley. La Salle claimed the entire area for France the next year and named it Louisiana.

The name "Chekagou," loosely translated to mean "wild onion," appeared on an 1684 map of the region. It was about 100 years before anything happened here after La Salle and Tonti.

Jean Baptiste Point du Sable, a French Canadian mulatto, established a trading post at the mouth of the Chicago River in 1779. In 1800, du Sable sold his property to **Jean Lalime**, another French Canadian.

Fort Dearborn was established on the south bank of the Chicago River, about where Michigan Ave. joins Wacker Dr. today, August 17, 1803, by **Capt. John Whistler** and a company of 40 men. It was named to honor Secretary of War Henry Dearborn.

John Kinzie arrived the next year and bought out Lalime, and became the leading civilian citizen in the fledgling settlement. He literally became the banker for the fort. He also sold liquor to the Indians which became a sore spot and created a certain amount of tension. Somehow in all this, Lalime, the man who sold out to Kinzie, became one of his principal adversaries.

In 1810, Captain Whistler was replaced as the post commander at Fort Dearborn by **Capt. Nathan Heald**. Lalime and Kinzie continued their differences until April 1812, when the two came to blows; and in the fight that followed, Kinzie stabbed Lalime to death. Kinzie, who had been wounded in the fight, fled but since no charges were brought against him, he soon returned.

Fort Dearborn was threatened at the outbreak of the War of 1812, and Captain Heald was ordered to abandon the fort by order of Gen. William Hull, from his headquarters in Detroit. As

Story of the Conley Print

The late Walter Conley, noted Chicago architect in the boom building days of the 1920s, became interested in producing a pictorial map of the village of Chicago on the day of its incorporation in 1833 for Chicago's Centennial in 1933.

Conley engaged research historians suggested by the Chicago Historical Society to uncover every possible piece of evidence about the Chicago landscape in 1833. The research effort took several years. The Conley Prints are believed to represent everything that is known about the physical makeup of Chicago at that time.

In early 1933, the work was completed. Four color stone plates were ordered in Germany, brought to Chicago and used to print 10,000 copies of Conley's map. In order to make certain there could never be more prints from the original plates, Conley destroyed them immediately after the pressrun.

Conley distributed some of his prized prints before he suffered a heart attack and was rushed to Mayo Clinic. He lived only a few months. His wife and son moved to Rochester to be near Mr. Conley. The family possessions, including the prints, were shipped to Rochester and stored. Later Mrs. Conley and her son moved to California several years after Walter's death.

In the mid-1950s one of the Conley Prints was discovered hanging in the Palmolive Building on North Michigan Ave. Another was found hanging in the Calumet Country Club. A search was made for Mrs. Conley to ascertain what had happened to the remaining Conley Prints. After months of searching Mrs. Conley was traced to a nursing home in California. She had forgotten about the prints but asked her son to go to Rochester to see if he could find the trunk she had left there.

The trunk was found. Time had taken its toll on the contents. Most of the prints were simply a single moldy chunk of rotten paper. Less than 2,000 were still in good condition and Mrs. Conley turned these over to Herbert R. Lewis, a good friend of the Conleys and one of the men who helped finance the project in 1933.

Upon his death, the remaining Conley Prints were sold to a private collector. Crossroads Communications, P. O. Box 7, Carpentersville, IL. 60110, today serves as an agent for the private collector. The firm will provide more information on how these prints may be obtained.

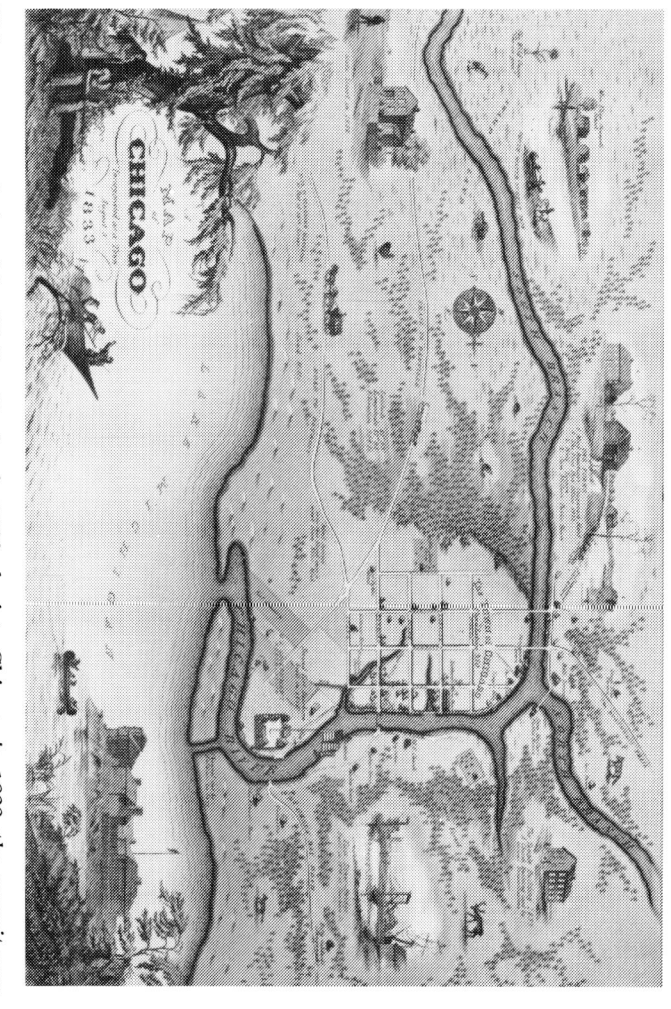

This map, commissioned by Walter Conley in 1933, depicts Chicago in 1833, the year it was incorporated by the Illinois legislature.

the small company of troops, accompanied by civilians, women and children, were leaving Friday, August 15, 1812, they were warned about the Indians in the area. As they reached a point, at 16th St. and Prairie Ave. today, Indians attacked and two women, 12 children and 28 soldiers were killed in the wagon train. The survivors were taken to Detroit where they were jailed by the British.

One man was not captured and stayed in Chicago. He was **Antoine Ouilmette**, who with his Indian wife had built their cabin next to the Kinzie place. John Kinzie and his family returned to Chicago in 1816. Fort Dearborn was rebuilt and reestablished in June, 1816, and Chicago began to grow and expand as a settlement. Fort Dearborn was finally abandoned in December, 1836.

Cholera struck the settlement in the early 1830s, brought to town by soldiers. Illinoisans from outside the area had flocked to Chicago during the Black Hawk War scare and set up tents which soon became unsanitary camps.

The town was platted in 1830; the plat map was published August 4. The three-eighths of a mile square was bounded by Halsted, Kinzie, State, and Madison Sts. The other nine streets were Des Plaines, Jefferson, Canal, Wells, La Salle, Dearborn, Lake, Randolph, and Washington. Each parcel, measuring 80 and 100 feet, was offered at no more than $70. It was also named county seat of newly established Cook County.

Gurdon Hubbard brought 400 hogs to Chicago to be butchered in 1829 and four years later built a huge packing plant and warehouse. By the late 1830s, Chicago-dressed pork was in demand in major cities in England. The Union Stock Yards were established on a 345 acre site between Halsted and 39th Sts. Christmas Day, 1865. At the time the yards could accommodate more than 100,000 head of cattle and hogs.

Rev. Jeremiah Porter, an Army Presbyterian chaplain at Fort Dearborn, established Chicago's first church, June 26, 1833. Within two years several other churches had been established by other denominations.

The city's first newspaper, the *Chicago Democrat*, began publishing in November, 1833. The *Daily Tribune* made its debut June 10, 1847 with **John T. Scripps** as its first editor. **Joseph Medill** arrived in Chicago in 1855 and became a partner in the Tribune. At the time there were nine daily newspapers serving the city.

It was Medill (1823-1899) who made the *Chicago Tribune* one

The 96-foot tall Douglas Tomb State Historical Site is located at 636 E. 35th St. in Chicago. Senator Stephen A. Douglas, a Democrat, was influential in Washington during the 1850s period.

of the world's most successful newspapers. He served as managing editor from 1855 to 1863, as editor from 1863 to 1866, and as publisher from 1874 until his death.

Six wards were created in the new city of Chicago in 1837. Out of each ward came an officer reporting to the High Constable.

A convicted rapist and murderer was hanged in 1840 in the city's first legal execution. **John Stone**, 34, a notorious loafer and troublemaker, was convicted of the rape and murder of **Mrs. Lucretia Thompson**, a Cook County farm wife. He was hanged Friday, July 10th.

The Lager Beer Riots of April 21, 1855, were created when the City Council increased the annual saloon license fee from $50 to $300. When the German saloonkeepers refused to pay the new license fee, **Mayor Levi D. Boone** ordered enforcement of the Sunday closing law. The saloonkeepers refused to obey the law. Two hundred saloonkeepers and bartenders were arrested and at their trial the judges were warned of impending rioting over the entire affair. On April 21 the riots began with warnings that 5,000 rioters planned to burn the City Hall and hang the mayor. In the fight that ensued several persons were injured and one killed. Fourteen men went on trial for rioting, two were convicted, none went to jail. The law on Sunday closing was shelved and saloonkeepers were no longer harrassed.

Cyrus H. McCormick (1809-84) arrived in Chicago in 1847 to set up a factory to manufacture the reaper he had developed and patented in 1834. Within two years after starting his plant here, McCormick was a millionaire.

It was in the 1850s that men like **Potter Palmer, Marshall Field**, and **Dwight L. Moody** arrived on the Chicago scene. Palmer, who became a successful businessman and was founder of the famous Palmer House hotel at State and Monroe Sts., arrived in 1852. Field, who founded the great department store that bears his name, came in 1856 from Massachusetts and began working for Palmer. Moody, the great evangelist, came to Chicago in 1856 seeking his fortune.

The population of the city in 1860 had reached 110,000. It was here that year that **Abraham Lincoln** was nominated as the Republican presidential candidate. This first national party convention in Chicago was held in a building, dubbed the Wigwam, at Lake and Market Sts. Lincoln's nomination came June 7, 1860.

Stephen A. Douglas (1813-61), who debated Abraham Lincoln on the slavery issue beginning in 1858 in their race for the

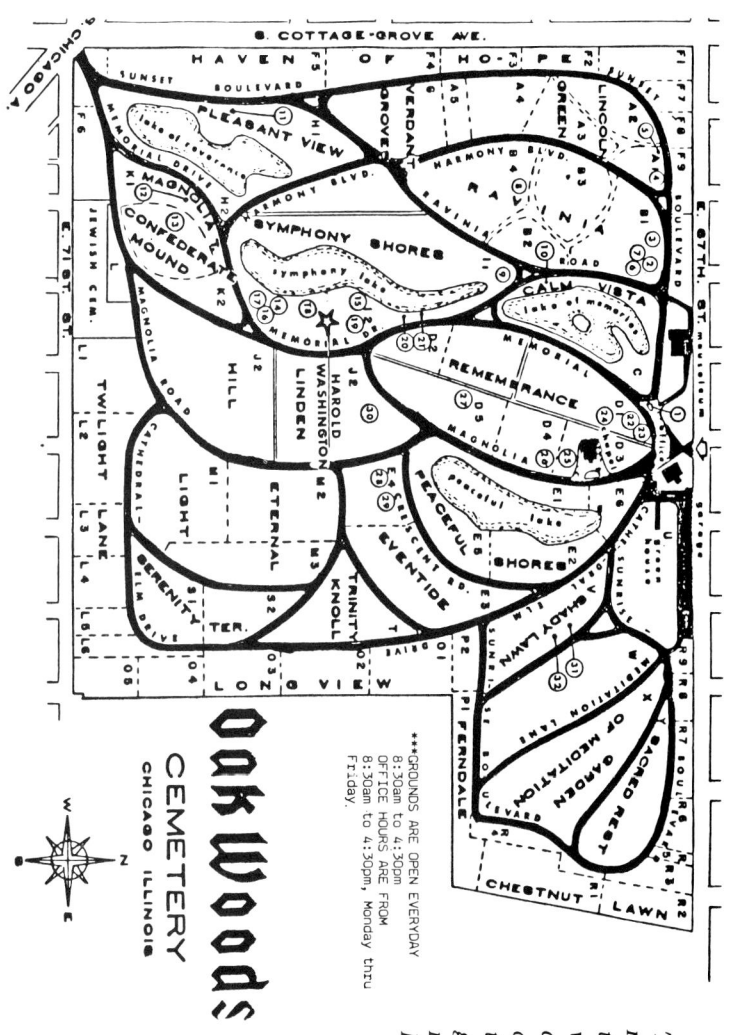

The Confederate Mound Memorial, honoring the more than 6,000 Confederate POWs who died at Camp Douglas during the Civil War, is located at Oak Woods Cemetery, 1035 E. 67th St. The graves are located in this mound area (in the lower left hand corner of this map).

This memorial in Oak Woods Cemetery on Chicago's South Side is located on the site of Camp Douglas, established as a POW camp during the Civil War. Over 6,000 Confederate soldiers died while imprisoned here. The names of the those buried on the site are listed on the memorial.

U.S. Senate, offered the principle of popular sovereignty in dealing with the question of slavery. He believed that the people of the territories should decide for themselves whether they wanted slavery. Lincoln, on the other hand, contended a nation half-slave and half-free could not exist. Douglas was one of three Democrats to run against Lincoln in 1860. He died in 1861, two months after the fall of Fort Sumter. The **Stephen A. Douglas Tomb and Memorial** are located in Douglas Tomb State Memorial Park on 35th St., east of Cottage Grove Ave. The memorial, completed in 1881 by Leonard Wells Volk, includes a 10-foot bronze figure of Douglas.

A tragedy on Lake Michigan in 1860 claimed 297 lives. The sidewheeler *Lady Elgin*, returning to Milwaukee from a trip to Chicago, Friday, September 7, was rammed by the schooner *Augusta* and sank.

Twenty-four year old **Col. Elmer E. Ellsworth**, a Chicagoan, was one of the first Union officers killed in the Civil War, emerging as a hero. Ellsworth had worked in Lincoln's Springfield law office in 1858. He was an expert on the Zouaves, the Berber troops of the French army, and outfitted his regiments in the Zouave uniform. He was killed by an innkeeper in Alexandria, Virginia, May 15, 1861, while hauling down a Confederate flag on the building.

Camp Douglas, on the South Side, was established as a Union POW camp during the Civil War. Out of the 20,000 Confederate prisoners held here, 6,129 died during the last three years of the war. Like the prison camps on both sides, Camp Douglas was a filthy place where starvation rations and little or no medical care of the sick and wounded created the appearance of a death camp.

Chicagoans mourned the death of Abraham Lincoln on April 15, 1865. Lincoln's body was brought to Chicago and lay in state in the courthouse rotunda in City Hall before being taken on to Springfield.

The **Great Chicago Fire of 1871** left 100,000 persons homeless with 250 to 500 persons burned to death. The wooden buildings of the day went up in flames quickly and 18,000 or more buildings were destroyed with losses estimated at more than $200 million. The fire is believed to have been started when **Mrs. Patrick O'Leary's cow** kicked over a lantern in the barn behind the family cottage at 137 DeKoven St. It started the evening of Sunday, October 8th, and only smouldering ashes remained by Tuesday. Within five years the city was rebuilt and began another

Chicago's famed Water Tower, on Michigan Ave., survived the Great Fire of 1871 and stands today as a monument to the survival of the city.

chapter in its life.

Marshall Field (1834-1906) established Marshall Field & Company in 1881, after buying out two partners. His slogan was "Give the Lady What She Wants," and he made special effort to get women in his store. He also brought several innovations into retailing that made his company very successful. Field gave 10 acres of ground as a site for the new University of Chicago and a contribution of $100,000 later. In 1893, he gave $1 million to establish a museum in Chicago and a later bequest of $8 million built the **Field Museum of Natural History**. Marshall Field built a home at 1905 Prairie Ave.

Marshall Field III and **Marshall Field IV**, grandson and great grandson of Marshall Field, became interested in the newspaper business and both became publishers. The grandson founded The *Chicago Sun* in 1941 and purchased control of the *Daily Times* in 1947, merging the two into the *Chicago Sun-Times*. His various enterprises were consolidated under Field Enterprises, Inc. He gave the 38-story Pittsfield Building in Chicago to the Field Museum of Natural History.

The great grandson built the Sun-Times building and purchased the *Chicago Daily News*. He succeeded his father as head of Field Enterprises, Inc., and in 1965 formed Field Communications Corporation and built *WFLD-TV, Channel 32*, which went on the air January 4, 1966. His son, **Marshall Field V**, became publisher of the *Sun-Times* and *Daily News* in 1969, filling the post his father held at the time of his death in 1965. The *Daily News* has since been closed and the *Sun-Times* sold to other interests. He is involved in several other enterprises.

Two great mail order companies emerged during the late 19th century—Montgomery Wards launched in 1872 by **A. Montgomery Ward** and his partner, **George R. Thorne**, and Sears Roebuck and Company 20 years later by **Richard W. Sears** and **Alvah C. Roebuck.**

The riot at Haymarket Square, between Halsted and Desplaines Sts., began on Tuesday, May 4, 1886. It had fomented over a period of time and involved workers and their grievances with Cyrus McCormick and other manufacturing plants. A union rally had been held the day before with the principal speaker being **August Spies**, a member of the Socialist Labor Party. When strikebreakers emerged from the nearby McCormick plant they were attacked. Police, led by **Capt. John Bonfield**, broke up the riot in which six police officers were injured, two seriously.

Photo by Ron Schramm/Chicago Convention and Visitors Bureau
Built in 1925, Gothic Revival skyscraper Tribune Tower is a Chicago landmark. The building features a large Gothic entrance as well as pieces of stone set around the base from famous buildings around the world. Pieces of Westminister Abbey, Cologne Cathedral and the Taj Mahal can be viewed.

Photo by Ron Schramm/Chicago Convention and Visitors Bureau

Dubbed the "Magnificent Mile," Michigan Avenue is home to one of the most exciting shopping districts in the world. This mile-long boulevard is between Wacker Drive and Oak Street. Shown here is the Water Tower Pumping Station, which was built in 1869. It was the only structure in the city to survive the Great Chicago Fire of 1871. Today, it stands in marked contrast to the beautiful modern architecture of the surrounding buildings.

Samuel Fielden, another union activist, was the speaker at the Tuesday rally. Just as he began his speech, the rains came along with Captain Bonfield and 180 officers. Bonfield demanded the meeting end and the crowd disperse. About this time a bomb was thrown into the police ranks and one officer was killed, six fatally wounded and 68 others injured. One rioter was killed, 12 wounded. Eight men were tried for the bombing. On June 20, 1886, seven—**August Spies, Michael Schwab, Samuel Fielden, Albert R. Parsons, Adolph Fischer, George Engel,** and **Louis Lingg**—were convicted and sentenced to be hanged. The eighth, **Oscar E. Neebe,** was sentenced to 15 years in prison. Lingg died of an explosion in his Cook County jail cell, November 10. The next afternoon, Spies, Parsons, Fischer, and Engel went to the gallows. In the meantime, the death sentences of Fielden and Schwab were commuted, and they were each given life sentences.

Moody Bible Institute, 820 N. La Salle, was founded by Dwight L. Moody (1837-99), the evangelist, in 1886. The institute offers a three-year college level program. He also established the interdenominational Moody Memorial Church and Moody Press in Chicago as well as a private high school for girls and another for boys in Massachusetts.

John Robert Gregg (1867-1948) invented the Gregg system of shorthand which was perfected in 1888. He founded a school in Chicago to teach his system.

George M. Pullman (1831-97) founded the Pullman Palace Car Company in 1867 after designing railroad sleeping cars for the Chicago & Alton Railroad with **Ben Field.** They designed the elaborate Pioneer sleeping car, introduced in 1865. The Pioneer was used in Lincoln's funeral train from Washington, D. C., to Springfield.

In 1880, Pullman established the town of Pullman, on the South Side, for his employees and labor problems soon followed. In 1882, Pullman reduced the transportation allowance of his employees and 1,000 workers went out on strike only to be fired. Over the next dozen years every striker was immediately fired. There were firings in 1884 when workers protested pay cuts and in 1885 1,400 porters lost their jobs when they struck for an eight hour work day. In the meantime, the railroad car baron's company town became part of Chicago (in 1889). By 1894, the workers became more united and first refused to handle Pullman cars on any rail line and then called a general strike against all the railroads. Troops were called in, and, in early July, riots broke

Photo by Ron Schramm/Chicago Convention and Visitors Bureau
Chicago's skyline viewed from the Chicago River. Shown here (left to right) is the Amoco Oil Building, the graceful, arc-shaped building at 333 N. Wacker Drive, and Sears Tower.

Photo by Ron Schramm/Chicago Convention and Visitors Bureau
Chicago is noted for its abundance of architectural styles, each adding to the magnificent skyline. Anchored by the John Hancock Center built in 1969, the Michigan Avenue area boasts a variety of landmark buildings as well as a world-class district.

out. Finally soldiers fired into a crowd, killing three children. Within the next few days, 13 more workers were killed and many others wounded to finally break the strike. It is estimated that in the violence of the strike, damages reached $80 million.

Eugene V. Debs (1855-1926), a native Indianan, formed the **American Railway Union** in 1893 and then ordered the strikes against Pullman and the railroads the next year. **President Grover Cleveland** ordered federal troops into Chicago to put down the strike against the railroads, declaring that it interfered with the mails. Debs was sentenced to a six month jail term for refusing to comply with a federal court injunction. He came out of jail a confirmed Socialist and ran for the presidency five times as a Socialist candidate. During World War I he made a speech condemning the war and was convicted under the Espionage Law in 1918 and sentenced to 10 years in prison. The sentence was commuted on Christmas Day, in 1921, by **President Warren G. Harding**.

Frances Elizabeth Caroline Willard (1839-98), educator and social reformer, served as president of the Evanston College for Ladies and was named dean of the college when it merged into Northwestern University in 1871. In 1879, she left the university to become president of the Woman's Christian Temperance Union (WCTU). Miss Willard was also a strong advocate of women's suffrage. A statue of Frances Willard represents the state of Illinois in Statuary Hall in the national capitol in Washington, D.C.

The WCTU was organized in 1874 in Cleveland, Ohio, with **Annie Wittenmyer** its first president. In 1883, Miss Willard founded the World's WCTU. Members of the WCTU believe in personal total abstinence from all alcoholic beverages and work for the abolition of all alcohol. WCTU national headquarters is located at 1730 Chicago Ave., Evanston.

Dr. Herman W. Mudgett, who called himself Henry H. Holmes, became known as the Monster of Sixty Third Street when it was learned he murdered at least 27 persons in the early 1890s. In 1892-93, he built a building 162 feet long, three stories high over a basement, across the street from a drug store that he had acquired under some unusual circumstances. "Holmes Castle," as it was called, contained 90 rooms with several torture chambers. It was charged that he burned some of his victims, others he killed when he sought to learn how much the human body could be stretched, and others were dissolved in acid vats.

His crimes surfaced in 1895 and he was charged with the murder of one, **Benjamin F. Pietzel**. The trial began October 28, 1895, and he was finally found guilty. Dr. Mudgett, alias Henry Holmes, was hanged May 7, 1896.

There have been other sensational crimes and mysteries.

Worldwide attention focused on the escape and disappearance of **Thomas "Terrible Tommy" O'Connor**, a thief and murderer. O'Connor was sentenced to be hanged for the murder of Detective **Patrick J. O'Neill**. Four days before he was to go to the gallows, he and three other prisoners escaped from the Cook County Jail. He was never found or heard of again .

In 1924, 13-year-old **Bobby Franks**, whose family lived in the exclusive Hyde Park area, was kidnapped and murdered by two brilliant University of Chicago students, **Nathan Leopold** and **Richard Loeb**. The case, known as the "Crime of the Century," drew nationwide headlines. The pair were given life sentences for the crime.

Dr. Alice Lindsay Wynekoop, a noted Chicago physician, was found guilty of murdering her daughter-in-law, November 20, 1933. Following a sensational trial, Dr. Wynekoop was sentenced to 25 years in prison and was paroled in 1946. She continued to vow that she would clear her name and name "the real killer." She died in a nursing home in 1955 and there were still many who wondered, "Did Dr. Alice really do it?"

University of Chicago freshman **William Heirens** was convicted and sentenced to prison for the murder of two women and six-year old **Suzanne Degnan**, whose dismembered body was discovered in North Side sewers. Heirens was the first inmate in a penal institution to earn a college degree.

The 1,000 Mile Horse Race or Chadron (Nebraska) to Chicago Cowboy Horse Race was held in 1893. The race began in Chadron at 5:45 p.m. on June 13, 1893, with nine riders competing in this endurance contest for horse and man. The winner, **John Berry**, arrived at the tent of **Col. William F. "Buffalo Bill" Cody** at his Wild West Show, playing adjacent to the Columbian Exposition grounds in Chicago, 9:30 a.m. June 27. The South Dakota cowboy was riding his horse Poison when he arrived at the Chicago finish line.

The first horseless carriage, an electric motorcar built by **William Morrison** of Des Moines, Iowa, made its appearance in downtown Chicago in 1891.

In 1895, **Herman H. Kohlsaat**, publisher of the *Chicago*

Times-Herald, sponsored the first auto race in America. Six self-propelled road vehicles entered the competition. The race, held Thanksgiving Day through an aftermath of a snow storm, covered the round trip from Chicago to Evanston. **Frank Duryea** won the race and $2,000 prize driving his **Duryea Motor Wagon**. The only other car to finish was a Mueller-Benz, imported from Germany.

The **World's Columbian Exposition**, celebrating the 400th anniversary of the first voyage of Columbus to the New World, was held in Chicago in 1893 during one of the worst depressions of that century. On the last day of the great fair, October 28, **Mayor Carter Harrison** was assassinated at his home by **Patrick E. Prendergast**, who had been denied a city post. Prendergast was hanged for the crime.

In 1900, the Chicago Sanitary and Ship Canal, connecting Lake Michigan with the Des Plaines River by way of the Chicago River, caused the Chicago River to flow backward, away from Lake Michigan.

The Car Barn Bandits, four young men from the slums—**Gustav Marx, Peter Niedemeyer, Emil Roeski** and **Harvey van Dine** —went on a crime spree including robbery and murder in 1903. They were finally captured late in the year after a gunfight in which a police officer was killed. They were tried in 1904 and hanged except for Roeski who was sentenced to life imprisonment.

A major tragedy claimed the lives of 602 persons, Wednesday, December 30, 1903, in the Iroquois Theatre fire. The fire was believed to have been caused by faulty wiring leading to a spotlight. The patrons attending the afternoon matinee panicked when they were unable to open the front doors because they swung inward instead of outward. The doors could not be opened because of the crush of theatregoers against them. To complicate matters, the side doors had been locked and most of the victims died of suffocation rather than burns. Several members of the "Mr. Bluebeard" cast and the theatre management and staff were arrested. The investigation continued for several weeks, however, no one was charged with any criminal act in the tragic fire.

Another tragedy occurred, July 24, 1915, when the *Eastland*, an excursion ship, fell over on its port side while at dockside near the Clark St. bridge and sank in 21 feet of water, killing 835 of its estimated 2,500 passengers. It was one of four ships chartered to take 7,000 Western Electric employees in Hawthorne on an ex-

Chicago Picasso, *by Pablo Picasso, is a 50-foot steel sculpture, an a abstact design from the head of a woman. It is located in Richard J. Daley Civic Center Plaza, Washington and Dearborn Sts.*

Gloria Swanson (1899-1983), a native Chicagoan, became a movie actress when she was only 15 years old. She made her first appearance in 1914 in a movie filmed at Essanay Studios on the outskirts of Chicago. This photo was taken in 1976.

cursion on Lake Michigan.

The first Rotary Club was organized in Chicago on February 23, 1905, by **Paul P. Harris**, a young attorney. Headquarters for Rotary International are located in Evanston.

The Elks (Benevolent and Protective Order of Elks) headquarters are in Elks National Memorial Building, 2750 Lakeview Ave. The building honors the Elks who served during World War I and II.

Westinghouse Corporation launched Chicago's first radio station, *KYW*, November 11, 1921. The studios were located in the Auditorium Theatre.

Several popular radio programs originated from Chicago in the 1920s and '30s. Among these were "Amos 'n' Andy," starring **Freeman Gosden** (Amos) and **Charles Correll** (Andy); "Fibber McGee and Molly," starring **Jim and Marian Jordan**; "Vic and Sade," with **Art Van Harvey** as Vic and **Bernadine Flynn** as Sade; and one of the long running soap operas, "The Guiding Light."

Chicago has had its share of race riots. In earlier years, blacks and whites were separated in numerous ways and there was always a certain amount of tension between the races. On July 27, 1919, a black youth swimming off the 27th Street beach, strayed into the area reserved for whites. When he tried to come ashore, he was stoned and forced back out into the lake where he drowned. The incident set off a major race riot that raged for four days, leaving 23 blacks and 15 whites dead and 500 persons injured. About 1,000 homes were also burned.

August 3, 1931, rioting broke out on the South Side when blacks and whites clashed over the eviction of a black family. The blacks abandoned a parade they were in and started a battle to prevent the legal eviction of a family living at 5016 S. Dearborn St. Three black rioters were killed and another seriously injured while three police officers were injured.

In April, 1968, riots broke out on the West Side in the aftermath of the assassination of Dr. Martin Luther King, Jr. Eleven persons were killed and damage was estimated at $10 million.

September 4, 1968, the Chicago police went on a rampage against demonstrators and innocent bystanders at and near the amphitheatre, scene of the Democratic national convention. There were several bloody clashes between demonstrators, many protesting the U.S. involvement in Vietnam, and police. No one was killed but many were injured. The three television networks

Richard J. Daley was elected mayor of Chicago in 1955 and served in the post until his death December 23, 1976. He served as chairman of the Cook County Democratic organization, attending many Democratic National Conventions, and was viewed by many as a kingmaker.

and a host of newspapers filed protests with the City of Chicago, the Governor of Illinois, and the National Committee of the Democratic Party over the treatment of newsmen and women covering the convention. They were particularly disturbed over the antics of **Mayor Richard Daley** and the Illinois delegation who blocked the aisles on the convention floor and created other disturbances. **Hubert Humphrey** was the Democratic presidential nominee emerging from this debacle.

Franklin D. Roosevelt was nominated for the presidency at the Democratic convention held in Chicago in 1932. His running mate was Texan **Jack Garner**. **Harold Ickes** (1874-1952), who worked as a Chicago newspaperman before becoming a lawyer, became one of the Roosevelt's confidants. He served in FDR's cabinet as U. S. Secretary of the Interior (1933-45) and also was appointed head of the Public Works Administration. He did not get along with President Truman and left his post at Interior in 1946.

Chicago **Mayor Anton J. Cermak** was killed by **Guiseppe Zangara**, a mentally ill bricklayer, February 15, 1933, while accompanying President-elect Franklin D. Roosevelt in Miami, Florida. It is believed Zangara was trying to assassinate Roosevelt. He was executed for killing Cermak, March 20, 1933.

The **Century of Progress Exposition** was held in Chicago in 1933-34. One of the features of the Exposition was the four-day visit of a fleet of Italian airplanes led by **Italo Balbo**, Benito

Mussolini's Minister of Air. The 24 seaplanes arrived in Chicago July 15, 1933, as one of the original 25 had crashed during a landing enroute. Balbo was presented the keys to the city by **Mayor Edward J. Kelly** and later was awarded the Distinguished Flying Cross from the U.S. Upon his return to Italy he was promoted to the rank of Air Marshal.

More than eight million dollars in damages resulted in the May 19, 1934, fire that destroyed a large section of the **Union Stock Yards** and the adjoining area. The fire covered over three square miles. Thousands of head of livestock were destroyed in the fire.

The **1937 Memorial Day Massacre** involved several hundred strikers and their sympathizers and non-striking employees of the Republic Steel Corporation on the South Side. The strikers had gathered outside the plant and were starting to set up a picket line when police arrived. In the melee that followed, the police opened fire and 10 men were killed and a number of others wounded. A Congressional investigation was held and concluded that the police were responsible for the fatal clash and had used "excessive force."

Samuel Insull (1859-1938) built a public utilities empire worth $3 billion by 1912. This empire crashed in 1932 and Insull fled the country. He was extradited in 1934 to face charges of using the mails to defraud investors and embezzlement. He was finally acquitted but not before losing his fortune along with several others who had invested with him. This scandal rocked Chicago because of its implications.

The first controlled atomic chain reaction was set off in the racquet court, under the old football stadium, at the University of Chicago, December 2, 1942. **Dr. Enrico Fermi**, assisted by **Walter Zinn** and **Herbert Anderson**, was in charge of this development, perhaps one of the most important in modern history. The atomic bomb was fully developed during the war and first used, August 6, 1945, on Hiroshima, Japan, where some 80,000 persons were killed. Chicago was the site of the Grebe shipyards which built several fighting ships for the U.S. Navy during World War II.

The Tucker automobile, designed and built by **Preston Tucker** (1903-56), was manufactured in a plant at 76th and Cicero Ave., on the South Side of Chicago from 1947-49. The car, said to be far ahead of its time, was capable of speeds up to 120 mph with gas mileage as high as 30 miles per gallon. Only 50 cars were built before money problems collapsed the enterprise.

Photo courtesy of the Daily Courier-News

Preston Tucker built 50 Tucker automobiles between 1947-49 in a plant on Chicago's South Side. Several of these cars are still in existence and two boys are shown here polishing up one of these for a Chicagoland auto show.

Chicago O'Hare International Airport was named in honor of World War II naval hero Lt. Edward "Butch" O'Hare in 1949.

The La Salle Hotel fire, of June 5, 1946, claimed the lives of 61 persons and the property damage amounted to millions of dollars.

Eighty-nine school children and three nuns were victims of a fire December 1, 1958, at Our Lady of The Angels School, 3808 W. Iowa St., on the Northwest Side. Many other students were hospitalized and treated for burns. It was believed the fire started in a stairwell.

By the 1950s, **Midway Airport** was the world's largest with over 900 flights daily. When **Charles Lindbergh** made the inaugural run of the St. Louis-to-Chicago airmail service in April, 1928, the airfield was little more than a pasture. Municipal Airport, as it was officially known, was created in 1927. The name was changed to Midway in 1949. The new Chicago O'Hare International Airport, 10 times the size of Midway, was opened to scheduled airline service in 1955.

Chicago's International Airport, the world's busiest today, is named in honor of **Lt. Cmdr. Edward H. "Butch" O'Hare**, a World War II hero. O'Hare, a St. Louis, Missouri, native, received the first Congressional Medal of Honor awarded to a serviceman in the U.S. Navy in World War II. He received the award for gallantry in action when he shot down five Mitsubishi bombers and seriously damaged a sixth in a nine plane formation that threatened O'Hare's aircraft carrier, the *U.S.S. Lexington*, on February 20, 1942. O'Hare went on to win the Navy Cross and Distinguished Flying Cross with one star before being shot down in a night battle off Makin, November 27, 1943.

This area has also produced 29 Congressional Medal of Honor recipients of its own. These include:

From the Civil War period were 1st Lt. John H. Fisher, Co. B, 55th Illinois Infantry; Pvt. George Ketsinger and Capt. Patrick H. White, both with the Chicago Mercantile Battery, Illinois Light Artillery; Cpl. John Warden, Co. E., 55th Illinois Infantry, all at Vicksburg, May 22, 1863; and Sgt. Thomas McGraw, Co. B, 23rd Illinois Infantry and Cpl. Patrick H. Highland, Co. D, 23rd Illinois Infantry, at Petersburg, Virginia, April 2, 1865.

During the Indian campaigns the recipients were Pvt. Christopher Freemeyer, Co. D, 5th U.S. Infantry, at Cedar Creek, Montana, from October 21, 1876 to January 8, 1877, and Pvt. James Sumner, Co. G, 1st Cavalry, in the Chiricahua Mountains, Arizona, October 20, 1869.

Sgt. Henry F. Schroeder, Co. L, 16th Infantry, received his

CMH at Carig, P.I., September 14, 1900.

World War I recipients were Cpl. Jake Allex, Co. H, 131st Infantry, 33rd Division, at Chipilly Ridge, France, August 9, 1918; 1st Sgt. Johannes S. Anderson, Co. B, 132nd Infantry, 33rd Division, Consenvoye, France, October 8, 1918; 1st Lt. Harold E. Goettler, 50th Aero Squadron, near Binarville, France, October 6, 1918; 1st Sgt. Sydney G. Gumpertz, Co. E, 132 Infantry, 33rd Division, in the Bois-de-Forges, France, September 29, 1918; Pfc Harold I. Johnson, Co. A, 356th Infantry, 89th Division, near Pouilly, France, November 9, 1918; Pvt. John J. Kelly, 78th Co., 6th Regiment, 2nd Division (USMC), at Blanc Mont Ridge, France, October 3, 1918 (also received the Navy Medal of Honor); and Pvt. Berger Loman, Co. H, 132nd Infantry, 33rd Division, near Consenvoye, France, October 9, 1918.

World War II recipients were T/Sgt. Robert E. Gerstung, Co. H, 313th Infantry, 79th Infantry Division, on the Siegfried Line near Berg, Germany, December 19, 1944; T/5 Eric G. Gibson, 3rd Infantry Division, near Isola Bella, Italy, January 28, 1944; Pfc Anthony L. Krotiak, Co. I, 148th Infantry, 37th Infantry Division, Balete Pass, Luzon, P.I., May 8, 1945; 1st Lt. Edward S. Michael, Air Corp, over Germany, April 11, 1944; Pfc Edward J. Moskala, Co. C, 383rd Infantry, 96th Infantry Division, at Kakazu Ridge, Okinawa, April 9, 1945; and Pfc Manuel Perez, Co. A, 511th Parachute Infantry, 11th Airborne Division, at Fort McKinley, Luzon, P.I., February 13, 1945.

The Korean Conflict recipients were Capt. Edward C. Kryzowski, Co. B, 9th Infantry Regiment, 2nd Infantry Division, near Tondul, Korea, August 31 to September 3, 1951, and Major Louis J. Sebille, USAF, near Hanchang, Korea, August 5, 1950.

Those fighting in Vietnam to receive the CMH were Sp. 4 Carmel B. Harney, Co. B, 1st Battalion, 5th Cavalry Division, in Binh Dinh Province, June 21, 1967; Sgt. Leonard B. Keller, Co. A, 3rd Battalion, 60th Infantry, 9th Infantry Division, Ap Bac Zone, May 2, 1967; Sgt. Allen J. Lynch, Co. D, 1st Battalion, 12th Cavalry, 1st Cavalry Division, December 15, 1967; Pfc Milton L. Olive, Co. B, 2nd Battalion, 503rd Infantry, 173rd Airborne Brigade, Phu Cuong, October 22, 1965; and Capt. Gerald O. Young, USAF, Southeast Asia, November 9, 1967.

The Navy and Marine Corps personnel from Chicago to receive the Congressional Medal of Honor were BM Willie Cronan, USN, while serving aboard the *U.S.S. Bennington* in an explosion at San Diego, July 21, 1905; Cpl. John P. Fardy, USMC, 1st Marine

Division, on Okinawa Shima in the Ryukyu Islands, May 7, 1945; Sgt. John H. Helms, USMC, serving aboard the *U.S.S. Chicago* saved a cook from drowning at Montevideo, Uruguay, January 10, 1901; Pvt. William C. Horton, USMC, in action against the enemy July 21 to August 17, 1900, Peking, China; 2nd Lt. John H. Leims, USMCR, 3rd Marine Division, at Iwo Jima, March 7, 1945; Capt. Joseph J. McCarthy, USMCR, 4th Marine Division, at Iwo Jima, February 21, 1945; and Lt. (jg) Weedon E. Osborne, Dental Corps, USN, 5th Marine Regiment, in combat at Bouresche, France, June 6, 1918.

Many of these awards were made posthumously.

Several entertainers were born and reared in Chicago. Among these were:

Edgar Bergen (1903-78), the ventriloquist whose acts included Charlie McCarthy and Mortimer Snerd, received a special Academy Award in 1937; **Jean Hagen** (1923-77), the actress, received the nomination in 1952 for the Best Supporting Actress in "Singing in the Rain;" and **Beulah Bondi** (1892-1981), the distinguished character actress, who received nominations for Best Supporting Actress for her part in "The Gorgeous Hussy" (1936) and "Of Human Hearts" (1938). Also in this group was **Robert Ryan** (1909-73), the actor, who received the nomination in 1947 for the Best Supporting Actor in "Crossfire."

Others include **John Agar**, born here in 1921 who became famous as Shirley Temple's first husband; **Sue Carol**, who married Alan Ladd; **Susanna Foster**, a movie songstress; **Blanche Sweet**, a protege of the great director D. W. Griffith; **John Vivyan**, the star of TV's "Mr. Lucky" series; and **Gayne Whitman** (1890-1958), who was radio's original "Chandu, the Magician."

Still others with Chicago connections, all actors or actresses were: Harry Antrim (1895-1967), Granville Bates (1882-1940), Rex Bell (1905-62), Alan Curtis (1909-53), Sidney D'Albrook (1886-1948), Dorothy Dalton (1893-1972), Frankie Darro (1918-76), Carter DeHaven Sr. (1886-1977), Dot Farley (1881-1971), Irene Fenwick (1887-1936), William "Billy" Franey (1885-1940), Louise Closser Hale (1872-1937), Burton Holmes (1870-1958), Helen Holmes (1892-1950), Stuart Holmes (1887-1971), Jessie Royce Landis (1904-72), Rod LaRocque (1898-1969), Fritz Leiber (1882-1949), Robert Z. Leonard (1889-1968), Richard Long (1927-74), Paul McGrath (1904-78), Lee Moran (1890-1961), Polly Moran (1883-1952), Gavin Muir (1907-72), Miriam Nesbitt (1873-

The noted poet, Carl Sandburg, (1878-1967) once lived at 4646 N. Hermitage in Uptown. Sandburg, born in Galesburg, worked as a newspaperman in Chicago from 1912 to the late 1920s. One of his best-known early poems was "Chicago" in 1914. Familiar famous faces in the early days of Uptown were film stars Charlie Chaplin, Gloria Swanson, and Ben Turpin. The old Essanay Studios were on Argyle.

1954), George Offerman Jr. (1912-63), Guy Oliver (1875-1932), Gertrude Olmstead (1904-75), Joan Peers (1911-75), Walter C. Percival (1887-1934), George Periolat (1876-1940), Paul Power (1902-68), Charles Richman (1865-1940), John Ridgely (1909-68), Gale Robbins (1922-80), Gail Russell (1924-61), Syd Saylor (1895-1962), Milton Sills (1882-1930), Myrtle Stedman (1881-1951), Larry Steers (1881-1951), Virginia Valli (1900-68), Mabel Van Buren (1878-1947), Bobby Vernon (1897-1939), Bruno Vesota (1922-76), Nella Walker (1886-1971), C. Denier Warren (1889-1971), and Bryant Washburn.

Among some of the Chicago writers and authors: **George Ade** (1866-1944), humorist and playwright; **Nelson Algren**, author of "The Man With the Golden Arm;" **Samuel Bellow**, who won the 1976 Nobel prize for literature; **Gwendolyn Brooks**, who won the Pulitzer Prize in 1950 for her collection of poems in "Annie Allen;" **James T. Farrell**, creator of the Studs Lonigan novels; **Willard Motley**, author of "Knock On Any Door" which was made into a movie starring Humphrey Bogart; **Ben Hecht**, who began his career in Chicago and wrote his first notable work, "Erik Dorn," in 1921 and went on to become famous as a playwright; and **Noel Gerson**, a prolific writer, who died November 20, 1988. His novels included "The Imposter," "The Forest Lord," "The Mohawk Ladder," "The Golden Eagle," "The Highwayman," "55 Days in Peking," and "The Naked Maja" which were made into movies. **Cornelia Otis Skinner** (1901-79) was a multi-talented performer and writer. She was not only an actress but an author, screenwriter, and playwright.

Other famous writers with connections to Chicago were **Carl Sandburg, Ring Lardner, Edgar Lee Masters, John O'Hara,** and **Vachel Lindsay.**

Harriet Monroe founded the magazine, *Poetry*, in 1912. Among the poets who contributed were Carl Sandburg, T. S. Eliot, Edna St. Vincent Millay, Robert Frost, James Joyce, D. H. Lawrence, and Edgar Lee Masters. By the time of Harriet Monroe's death in 1938, her magazine had become world-famous.

Jazz has always been popular in Chicago and many of the great jazz musicians either were natives or gained their musical reputations in clubs here. A partial list of some of these musicians includes such names as Arthur "Rip" Bassett, Wallace Henry "Bish" Bishop, Albert W. "Happy" Coldwell, Israel Crosby, Benny Goodman, Gene Krupa, Jimmy Lord, Joseph Francis "Joe" Marsala, "Skip" Morr, Frank Orchard, Ben Pollack, Gil Rodin, and Cassino Wendell Simpson.

Photo by Ron Schramm/Chicago Convention and Visitors Bureau
A skyline view of the Windy City. Chicago boasts three of the five tallest buildings in the United States. The Sears Tower ranks first, followed by fourth and fifth tallest Standard Oil building and the John Hancock buildings, respectively.

THE ILLINOIS STATE TREE
The Illinois State tree is the White Oak.

A flowering crabapple tree frames the skyline of Chicago in this early springtime photograph. The 109-story Sears Tower (hidden in the photo) dominates the city's skyline. It is the largest private office complex in the world, containing 4.4 million square feet with 101 acres of floor space. The black aluminum skin and bronze-tinted glass skyscraper has afforded spectacular views of the Windy City from its Skydeck since 1974.

Chapter 4
The Gangster Era

The mob came to Chicago early and has been part of the city's colorful past and present. The open warfare between rival gangs became front page news in the 1920s and '30s.

A glimpse of the hoodlums who controlled the Windy City more than a half century ago are here. Presented are stories of Al "Scarface" Capone, George "Bugs" Moran, Big Jim Colosimo, John Dillinger, and George "Baby Face" Nelson.

Chapter 4
The Gangster Era

Chicago's gangster era emerged and flourished in the 1920s and '30s. Names like Al "Scarface" Capone, George "Baby Face" Nelson, George "Bugs" Moran and John Dillinger are among a few of the names that come to mind when reflecting on that era. There were others just or almost as notorious.

Al Capone, born in Naples, Italy, in 1899, landed in New York when he reached America. He moved to Chicago in 1918 and became a lieutenant to **John Torrio**, one of the most feared gangsters in the Windy City. Torrio succeeded **Big Jim Colosimo**, the first leader of the syndicate, who was killed May 11, 1920, behind his popular South Wabash Avenue restaurant.

Torrio established "speakeasies" during Prohibition but after several murders he fled the city to return to Italy in the midtwenties and Capone quickly took control to become the third leader of the Chicago syndicate. He became implicated in several murders and was known to receive tribute from businessmen and politicians. His crime syndicate controlled gambling and vice and, in 1927 alone, his income was estimated at over $100 million.

Capone received the nickname "Scarface" for the three scars on the left side of his face. He received the knife wounds at the hands of **Frank Galluccio**, a tough hood, during a fight over a girl in a Brooklyn bar in 1917. He had two older brothers, who landed in Chicago. Frank was killed in a battle with the police in Cicero in 1924. The other brother, Ralph J. "Bottles," became a minor boss in the Chicago underworld. He died of natural causes in 1974.

Assistant States Attorney William McSwiggin, who had gained the reputation as a crime fighter, was killed with two others, April 27, 1926, outside the Pony Inn in Cicero. Capone was believed to have been the triggerman.

The tenacles of the gangland boss reached everywhere. **Jake Lingle**, the *Chicago Tribune's* police reporter, was on Capone's payroll, for example. No one mentioned the fact that Jake's lifestyle was far greater than his reporter's salary could possibly stretch. It is claimed that Lingle set the prices of beer in Chicago and controlled graft in connection with dog racing in the late '20s. While walking to the Illinois Central suburban train station,

June 9, 1930, Jake Lingle was shot in the head. **Leo Brothers**, a St. Louis hood, was convicted of the killing and sentenced to 14 years in prison.

During the first four months of 1926, there were 29 gangland murders in Chicago and by 1930 over 200 murders had been committed, with no one arrested and convicted. Capone's headquarters during this period was the Metropole Hotel, 2300 S. Michigan Ave., where he occupied 50 rooms on two floors. He maintained offices in a nearby hotel connected to the Metropole by an underground tunnel. Capone also lived from time to time at the Four Deuces Brothel, 2222 S. Wabash; a residence at 7244 S. Prairie; and in a summer home in Mercer, Wisconsin.

The heart of the bootleg brewery business in that era was at Oak and N. Cleveland in Chicago. Somewhere between 15 and 40 gang-ordered killings occurred on the corner of these two streets. Gang chief **Antonio Lombardo**, with two bodyguards at his side, was shot down near State and Madison, the city's busiest intersection.

Capone dispatched those members of the gang who he regarded as a threat. First, **Charles Dion "Deanie" O'Banion** (1892-1924), whose territory was the North Side, was murdered by three gunmen, November 8, 1924, in his flower shop at 738 North State St., across from Holy Name Cathedral, where he had served as an altar boy and in the choir. He was buried in Mount Carmel Cemetery. O'Banion, born and raised on Chicago's North Side, formed his gang at the outset of Prohibition with Bugs Moran as one of the members. Opposed to prostitution, O'Banion kept it out of his North Side territory. He ran Chicago's 42nd Ward while alive and in power.

O'Banion's chief lieutenant, **Hymie Weiss**, swore vengeance. He made his headquarters in the O'Banion flower shop. On October 11, 1926, he was killed by machine gun fire as he entered the shop. O'Banion's other lieutenant, **Vincent Drucci**, was killed by a police officer. The only member of the gang remaining was **Bugs Moran**, who outlived Capone. He died in 1957.

Weiss became a problem for Capone as he continued to shoot his friends and allies. September 20, 1926, an 11-car cavalcade drove into the heart of Capone's territory, in Cicero, and riddled the Hawthorne restaurant with machine gun bullets, where Capone was having lunch. Earlier, on January 12, 1925, Weiss, with Bugs Moran and **Schemer Drucci**, pulled alongside Capone's car at State and 55th St. and opened fire, wounding the driver.

Scarface had gotten out of the car moments before Weiss arrived on the scene. Capone sought a truce between the rival gangs but all Weiss wanted was O'Banion's killers. Capone declined to hand over the triggermen and instead posted some of his gunmen in a rented room across from the flower shop. It was from this vantage point that they gunned down Weiss.

Weiss and Drucci were involved in the two 1926 Battles of The Standard Oil Building, at 910 S. Michigan Ave. The first occurred August 10, when the pair arrived at the building to payoff a ward boss. Four Capone gunmen charged them and began shooting but neither Weiss or Drucci were hit and the would-be assassins escaped. Five days later, as Weiss and Drucci were driving by the Standard Oil Building, a car pulled up and opened fire on them. Again they escaped.

Sam "Smoots" Amatuna (1898-1925) was one of Chicago's most colorful and brutal gangsters in the 1920s. Smoots was noted for carrying his weapons in musical instrument cases. He also ran afoul of Al Capone when he took control of Unione Siciliane in 1925. Scarface had planned for this post to fall to one of his lieutenants. Amatuna was killed on Capone's orders while being shaved in a Cicero barbershop, November 13, 1925.

The **Terrible Gennas**, brothers Bloody Angelo, Tony the Gentleman, Mike the Devil, Pete, Sam, and Jim, were in the bootlegging business. They threatened other Chicago mobs and finally had to be dealt with. Angelo, Tony and Mike were killed by rival gang members, in early 1925, to break up the family gang. The other three brothers disappeared but returned much later to operate legitimate businesses.

John Scalise and **Albert Anselmi**, both murderers, were first hired by the Gennas but double crossed them to join Capone. Capone, who thought they were plotting against him, had them killed, May 27, 1929. They were clubbed to death with baseball bats at a party thrown by Scarface.

Capone traveled about Chicago in a seven-ton bulletproof car with combination locks so no one could open it to plant a bomb inside. His numerous bodyguards dressed in tuxedos when the boss went to a theatre or elegant restaurant. Several attempts were made on his life.

Eliott Ness (1902-57) and his team of "The Untouchables" arrived on the scene in 1928 and were assigned to harrass Capone's gang. Ness headed a ten-man law enforcement team, each man selected because he could not be corrupted. A University of Chicago graduate, Ness loved the publicity and his reputation and that of "The Untouchables" became bigger than life. After Capone's fall, Ness became the Justice Department's chief investigator of Prohibition violations in the Chicago area.

Another mob-related scandal was the 1928 (Republican) "Pineapple Primary." The use of "pineapples" (the gangster's term for bombs) became widespread to intimidate both voters and office seekers. The Republican opponents were **Sen. Charles S. Deneen** and **Mayor William Hale "Big Bill" Thompson**. Capone supported the Thompson faction and used "muscle" in the campaign that saw the homes of rivals bombed and several campaign workers killed. Among those killed in one bombing episode was cafe owner and racketeer **Diamond Joe Esposito**, March 21, 1928.

Among the most noted of the Chicago terrorist bombers was **Jim Sweeney**, believed to have organized the first gang of bombers in the U.S., convicted in 1921 and sentenced to a long term in Joliet prison. Another was **Joseph Sangerman**, believed to have killed several persons involved in the city's labor battles in the early '20s. He was convicted of bombings in 1925 and sent to prison.

James Belcastro was a leader of the Black Hand extortion racket in Chicago. He became a trusted terrorist for Al Capone and specialized in blowing up saloons, with their customers, whose owners refused to buy Capone's beer. Belcastro, whom the Chicago underworld called the "King of the Bombers," planted explosives at voting places and outside the homes of political rivals of Mayor Thompson during the 1928 Chicago primary. The terrorist died of natural causes at a ripe old age.

Joseph Aiello (1891-1930), with his brothers Dominick, Antonio, and Andrew, were enemies of Al Capone and tried on several occasions to have him assassinated. Finally, Aiello offered $50,000 for Capone's head forcing him to retaliate. Joe Ailleo was shot to death on N. Kolmar Avenue by Capone's hit men, October 23, 1930.

Capone was indicted for tax invasion in 1931 by a federal grand jury and was convicted and sentenced to an 11-year prison term. In 1939, physically and mentally shattered, he was released. He died in 1947 and was buried in Mt. Carmel cemetery in Hillside. (The headstone was stolen from the grave in 1972).

Seven of Bugs Moran's henchmen were killed by other mobsters posing as police officers at 2122 N. Clark St. in the bloody

The first "Blue Moon," in the mid-1930s, was a lounge in Elgin said to have been frequented by Al "Scarface" Capone. Today it is a popular restaurant and nightclub.

St. Valentine's Day massacre of February 14, 1929. Those killed were found in the rear room of the S.M.C. Cartage Company building owned by **James Clark**, one of those killed. The other victims were **Peter** and **Frank Gusenberg, Arthur Hayes, Frank Foster, Al Weinshank,** and **John May**. It was believed the murders were ordered in retaliation for an earlier liquor hijacking by the Moran gang. **Jack "Machine Gun" McGurn** (1904-36), suspected as Capone's hit man in the St. Valentine's Day murders, was killed, February 13, 1936, by gang members at a bowling alley at 805 Milwaukee Ave. McGurn was an alias for James DeMora. During his tenure with Capone he is credited with killing 28 men.

Before he was 21 years old, Bugs Moran (1893-1957) had committed 21 robberies and served three jail sentences. He became one of "Deanie" O'Banion's lieutenants and was a killer. His end finally came when he was arrested for robbing an Ohio bank messenger in 1946. He was sent to prison for this crime and died of cancer in Leavenworth in 1957.

Frank Nitti, appointed as Capone's chief of operations when he was sent to prison, committed suicide in 1943 as he faced a prison term for tax evasion. Nitti, called "The Enforcer," had served an 18-month prison term in the early 1930s for tax violations. **Paul "The Waiter" Ricca** (1897-1972) took control of the mob about 1940. He was convicted of extortion and sentenced to 10 years in prison but was paroled in 1947. He died of natural causes in Chicago in 1972.

John Dillinger (1902-34) was a Indiana bank robber who operated out of Chicago. After an attemped bank robbery he was paroled and, in 1933, organized a gang that terrorized the Midwest for the next several months. His first bank robbery occurred July 17, 1933, at Daleville, Indiana, where he and his gang got only $3,000. He escaped from jail twice and was responsible, directly or indirectly, for 16 killings. By 1934 he had been declared "Public Enemy Number 1" by the G-Men. By the summer of 1934, he and his gang had taken $302,739 in bank robberies.

His career and life came to an abrupt end in July, 1934. He was killed as he and "the girl in red," 42-year old **Anna Sage**, emerged from the Biograph Theatre, 2433 N. Lincoln Ave. Federal agents, led by **Melvin Purvis**, sprung their trap at 10:40 p.m. Three bullets hit Dillinger and he died of his wounds enroute to Alexian Brothers' hospital. Mrs. Sage lived just around the corner from the theatre, at 2420 N. Halsted. Dillinger's

Bank Robber John Dillinger was declared "Public Enemy Number One" by the G-Men in early 1934.

Headlines like these in the Elgin newspaper in July 1934 announced the end of the notorious John Dillinger.

These four mechanics were believed to have worked on Al Capone's automobiles. The only one identified was George "Don" Clark (on the right) from Blue Island. They are shown here in a Chicago garage in the early '30s.

family claimed the body and he was buried in the Crown Hill Cemetery in Indianapolis.

He was succeeded as "Public Enemy Number 1" by **George "Baby Face" Nelson** (1908-34), an alias for Lester M. Gillis. Born and reared in Chicago, he was a "mad dog" killer. Only five feet five inches tall, Gillis wanted to be known as "Big George" Nelson. As a teenager he was sentenced twice to St. Charles (Ill.) School for Boys for auto theft. By 1929 he had earned a tough reputation while working for Capone. In 1931, he was captured while robbing a bank and sentenced to prison from a year to life. He escaped in 1932 while being returned to prison after testifying against an associate in a Wheaton courtroom and immediately joined up with Dillinger.

About 4 p.m. November 27, 1934, two federal agents spotted Nelson, his wife, **Helen Gillis**, and another man, driving on Northwest Highway near Barrington, Ill. They gave chase and exchanged shots with one of the bullets disabling Nelson's car. In the shoot-out that followed on the streets of Barrington, Nelson was hit 17 times. Both officers, **Samuel P. Crowley** and **Herman E. Hollis**, were fatally wounded. Nelson and his companions escaped in the agents' bullet-riddled car, found the next morning in a ditch in Winnetka. His wife had taken him to a house "somewhere near Chicago," after the shooting where he died. Nelson's body, clad only in his undergarments, was found in a ditch in Niles Center, Ill. His wife was immediately tabbed "Public Enemy Number 1" but was taken into custody two nights later. Only three mourners attended Nelson's funeral. The burial was in St. Joseph Cemetery in River Grove, Ill. Helen Gillis was returned to prison in Wisconsin.

Bootleg king **Roger "the Terrible" Touhy** (1898-1959) controlled Des Plaines in the northwest section of Cook County. There were six Touhy brothers and Roger was the boss. He was arrested in 1934 for the alleged kidnapping of **Jake "the Barber" Factor**, an international con man with ties to Capone. His first trial ended in a hung jury, however, in the retrial he was convicted and sentenced to 99 years in Joliet prison. In 1942, he escaped but was recaptured a short time later and sentenced to another 99-year prison term. Touhy was released from prison in 1959—23 days later to be gunned down on the steps of his sister's house at 125 N. Lotus.

Gangland type killings in Chicago continue annually. In 1960 there were eight such killings; in 1961, 15; in 1962, 14; in 1963, six; in 1964, four; and in 1965, seven.

The mob is still active although not as violent as it once was. Corruption still abounds. Big time crime is more sophisticated but continues to flourish. It is all part of Chicago's colorful history.

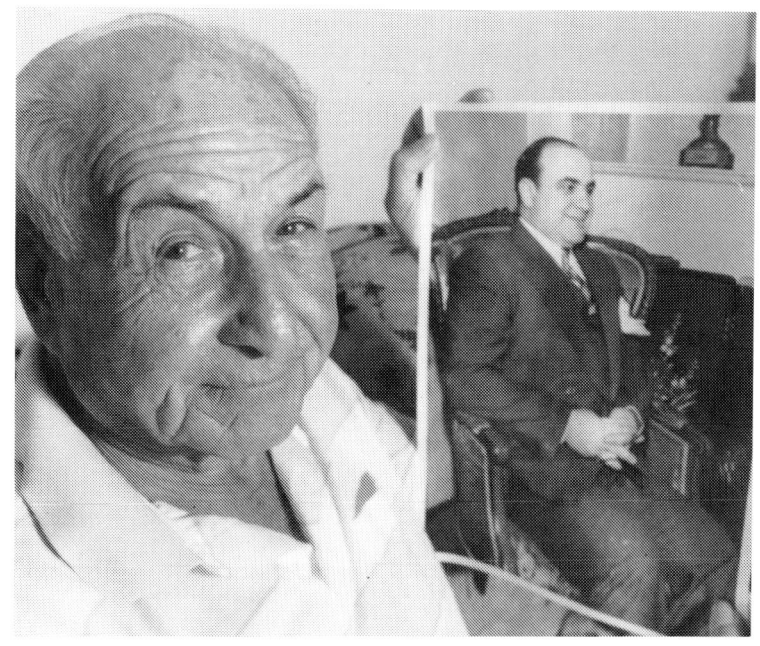

Courtesy Daily Courier-News, Elgin

Tony Berardi, a photographer for The Evening American in Chicago during the reign of mob boss Al Capone, is retired and lives in San Diego. He was the first photographer at the scene of the St. Valentine Day's massacre in 1929. Berardi is shown here with one of his many photos of Capone he took during his decade of covering the gangster and his hoodlums. His city editor sent him to Capone's headquarters in the Lexington Hotel offices to take a portrait of the gangster.

Chapter 5
Chicago Museums and Historical Sites

Chicago boasts some of the world's most renown museums. This chapter lists the active museums and galleries in 1989.

Museum Listings and Historic Sites
Adler Planetarium
American Police Center and Museum
Art Institute of Chicago
Balzekas Museum of Lithuanian Culture
Buckingham Fountain
Chicago Academy of Sciences
Chicago Architecture Foundation
Chicago Board of Trade
Chicago Historical Society
Chicago Maritime Museum
Chicago Mercantile Exchange
Copernicus Cultural and Civic Center
DuSable Museum of African History
Field Museum of Natural History
Grand Army of the Republic Museum
Here's Chicago
Historic Pullman Foundation
International Museum of Surgical Sciences
Jane Addams' Hull House
John G. Shedd Aquarium
Mexican Fine Arts Center
Morton B. Weiss Museum of Judaica, K.A.M.
Museum of Broadcast Communications
Museum of Contemporary Art
Museum of Contemporary Photography
Museum of Holography
Museum of Science and Industry
Oriental Institute of University of Chicago
Peace Museum
Polish Museum of America
Printers Row Printing Museum
Robie House
Spertus Museum of Judaica
Swedish American Historical Society
Swedish American Museum
Terra Museum of American Art
Telephony Museum
Tribune Tower
Ukrainian National Museum
Vietnam Museum

Chapter 5
Chicago Museums

Several of the nation's largest and most popular museums—the Art Institute of Chicago, Field Museum of Natural History, the Adler Planetarium, Shedd Aquarium, and the Museum of Science and Industry—are located in Chicago. There are many others.

Among the attractions located in the Grant Park area: BUCKINGHAM FOUNTAIN, in Grant Park between Congress Dr. and Columbus Dr. on Lake Shore Dr., is one of the largest fountains in the world. Built in 1927, the fountain rises to 135 feet. Fountain displays are held daily throughout the summer, 11:30 a.m. to 9 p.m., with a color light display from 9 to 10 p.m.

FIELD MUSEUM OF NATURAL HISTORY, Roosevelt Rd. at Lake Shore Dr., was founded in 1893 during the World's Columbian Exposition by **Marshall Field** and other civic leaders. It was originally housed in the Palace of Fine Arts building following the world's fair. In 1921 it was moved to its present location in Grant Park and is listed on the National Register of Historic Places. The museum claims more than 19 million artifacts and specimens in its collections.

The story of man, the animal and plant worlds, and the Earth can be explored in the exhibits placed on three floors. The museum is probably best known for its displays of dinosaurs, fossils, Egyptian mummies, and American Indian artifacts.

Field Museum is open 9 a.m. to 5 p.m. daily. An admission is charged.

JOHN G. SHEDD AQUARIUM, 1200 S. Lake Shore Dr., was opened in 1930 as a gift to the people of Chicago from **John Graves Shedd**, president and chairman of the board of Marshall Field & Company. It is the world's largest indoor aquarium. More than 6,000 freshwater and marine animals are displayed in 200 naturalistic habitats.

The intricate beauty of a Caribbean reef is re-created in the 90,000-gallon Coral Reef Exhibit where divers hand-feed sharks, sea turtles and other fish daily at 11 a.m. and 2 p.m.

The Shedd Aquarium is open 9 a.m. to 5 p.m. daily, March through October; 10 a.m. to 5 p.m. daily, November through February. It is closed Christmas and New Year's Day. An admission

Photo by Ron Schramm/Chicago Convention and Visitors Bureau

Buckingham Fountain, located in Grant Park, is one of the largest in the world. Modeled after a fountain in Versailles, it has a central stream with 133 jets of water, some of which reach about 200 feet. Each evening in May-September, the fountain is illuminated with shifting colors from 9 to 10. Buckingham Fountain was donated to Chicago in 1922 by Kate Buckingham. Facing Grant Park is the Amoco Oil Building. The 80-story building is the third tallest building in the city.

This map spots three of Chicago's noted tourist attractions, all within easy walking distance of one another. These include the Field Museum of Natural History, Shedd Aquarium, and Adler Planetarium.

Courtesy, Field Museum of Natural History
One of the many mastodon exhibits at the Field Museum of Natural History. This world noted museum was founded in 1893.

The Shedd Aquarium (above) and Adler Planetarium (below) are located just off Lake Shore Dr. in Chicago.

The exterior of Chicago's Field Museum is closely patterned after the Erechtheium, one of the Athenian Acropolis temples. Field Museum's present structure was designed by Daniel Burnham, the renowned Chicago designer and city planner. The building is constructed of white Georgian marble. Eight caryatids, created by Henry Hering, embellish the exterior and interior of the museum.

The Terra Museum of American Art at 666 N. Michigan Ave.

is charged, except on Thursday when admission is free.

ADLER PLANETARIUM, 1300 S. Lake Shore Dr., was founded by **Max Adler**, a Sears, Roebuck and Company executive, in 1930, the first planetarium constructed in the western hemisphere. It is a leader in the field of astronomy. In addition to its sky shows it has one of the world's finest collections of early astronomical and navigational instruments. The Planetarium's featured attraction is the two-part, multi-image Sky Show.

Adler Planetarium is open 9:30 a.m. to 4:30 p.m., Monday through Thursday; 9:30 a.m. to 9 p.m., Friday; 9:30 a.m. to 5 p.m. weekends and holidays, September 1 through June 15; and 9:30 a.m. to 5 p.m. Saturday through Thursday; and 9:30 a.m. to 9 p.m. Friday, June 16 through August 31. It is closed on Thanksgiving and Christmas. Admission to the planetarium is free. Admission is charged for the sky shows. For further information, call 322-0300.

HERE'S CHICAGO, located in the Water Tower Pumping Station just across the street from the landmark Water Tower, Michigan Ave. and Pearson St., presents moving exhibits and a 45-minute sight and sound presentation about Chicago. City and area tours also are operated from this center. The 45-minute show is presented every hour and half hour starting at 10 a.m. Doors open at 9:30 a.m. Admission is charged for the presentation.

CHICAGO MARITIME MUSEUM, North Pier Chicago, 455 E. Illinois St., opened the summer of 1989. The focus of Chicago's first maritime museum will be the role of the Port of Chicago in the development of the midwest, taking the visitor from the days of the French voyageurs, who discovered the crucial Chicago portage to the West, to today's international shipping and recreational port. A gift shop and library will also welcome visitors. Call 836-4343 for information on hours, admission and current exhibits.

TERRA MUSEUM OF AMERICAN ART, 666 N. Michigan Ave., was founded in Evanston in 1980 by Ambassador **Daniel J. Terra**, a collector of 19th and 20th century American art. The museum has hosted a vast array of exhibitions since moving to Chicago in 1987.

Terra Museum is open 12 noon to 8 p.m. Tuesday; 10 a.m. to 5 p.m. Wednesday through Saturday; and 12 noon to 5 p.m. Sunday and is closed on Monday. It is closed New Year's, July 4th, Thanksgiving, and Christmas. An admission is charged. Children

Courtesy, Field Museum of Natural History

Children are enthralled by this exhibit of prehistoric people at the Field Museum of Natural History, one of the world's great museums.

Exhibits at the Field Museum on Chicago's lakefront.

Other popular exhibits at the Field Museum.

Indian displays on exhibit at the Field Museum.

The landmark Water Tower Pumping Station, Michigan Ave. and Pearson St., serves as a travel and entertainment center featuring the sights and sounds of Chicago. A 45-minute "The Best Show About Town" takes one into the past to experience the recreation of the infamous Gangster Era and the Great Chicago Fire. Open 9:30 a.m. to 5 p.m. Sunday through Thursday and 9:30 a.m. to 6 p.m. Friday and Saturday. An admission is charged.

under the age of 12 are admitted free.

TRIBUNE TOWER, 435 N. Michigan Ave., was completed in 1925 and is a 36-story skyscraper. On the south side of the building, facing Pioneer Court, are copper engravings of the Tribune's front pages over the 100 year period, 1863-1963. The outside walls of the building contain fragments from historic sites from all over the world. For example, the front entrance, contains mementos from the Alamo, the Great Wall of China, and Westminister Abbey.

GRAND ARMY OF THE REPUBLIC MEMORIAL MUSEUM, Chicago Public Library Cultural Center, 78 E. Washington St., features a collection of artifacts, photographs and manuscripts pertaining to the Civil War and American history. The annual Civil War exhibit is one of the museum's highlights. It is open 9 a.m. to 7 p.m. Monday through Thursday, 9 a.m. to 6 p.m. Friday, and 9 a.m. to 5 p.m. Saturday. Admission is free.

MUSEUM OF CONTEMPORARY PHOTOGRAPHY, Columbia College, 600 S. Michigan Ave., presents a wide range of provocative exhibitions in recognition of photography's many roles—as a medium for communication and artistic expression, as a documenter of life and the environment, as a commercial industry, and as a powerful tool in the service of science and technology. In addition, special exhibitions are prepared in collaboration with other art institutions to combine photographic essays with other forms of art and investigate the medium's interrelationships with art and culture. Related programs of the museum include a Permanent Collection and Print Study Room, lectures and panel discussions, traveling exhibitions originated by the museum, publications, and a Museum Studies program, sponsored by the Department of Photography at Columbia College. It is open 10 a.m. to 5 p.m. weekdays and 12 noon to 5 p.m. Saturday, September through May; closes one hour earlier during the months of June and July and is closed to the public during the month of August. Admission to the exhibitions is free; there is a charge for lectures.

ART INSTITUTE OF CHICAGO, Michigan Ave. and Adams St., was founded in 1879 by some of Chicago's leading citizens. Among its most treasured possessions are El Greco's "The Assumption of the Virgin," Rembrandt van Rijin's "Officer with a Gold Chain," Paul Cezanne's "The Basket of Apples," Mary Cassat's "The Bath," Pablo Picasso's "The Old Guitartist," Grant Wood's "American Gothic," Edward Hopper's "Nighthawks,"

The Bezalel Ark displayed in the Spertus Museum was planned and designed in 1913 and completed in 1923. It is one of many exhibits in the museum that preserve and interpret Jewish history and culture.

and Francois Auguste Rene Rodin's sculpture of "Adam."

An unusual and large collection of weapons and defensive armament is included in the Harding Collection of Arms and Armor. Another unique collection is the 68 Thorne Miniature Rooms constructed in 1937 and 1949 commissioned by Mrs. James Ward Thorne. The miniatures, with a scale of one inch to a foot, include European interiors dating from the 13th century and American interiors from the 17th century to the 1930s.

The museum's collections span 40 centuries of human creativity. It has a wide range of collections presented in unusual and unique exhibits.

The Art Institute is open 10:30 a.m. to 4:30 p.m. Monday, Wednesday, Thursday and Friday; 10:30 a.m. to 8 p.m. Tuesday; 10 a.m. to 5 p.m. Saturday; and 12 noon to 5 p.m. Sunday. An admission is charged.

SPERTUS MUSEUM OF JUDAICA, 618 S. Michigan Ave., was established at Spertus College of Judaica in 1967. It is devoted to the acquistion, preservation and interpretation of Jewish history and culture, and its collection includes art and artifacts from around the world. Its permanent collection consists of: ceremonial objects, archaeological artifacts, textiles, numismatics, paintings, sculpture, and other examples of fine art. Its art collections include works by Phillip Pearlstein, Abraham Ratner, Andy Warhol, Eliel Saarinen, and Freidrich Adler. It is the purpose of the museum to transmit the Jewish legacy to Jewish and non-Jewish visitors through special exhibitions and educational programming. The Paul and Gabriella Rosenbaum ArtiFact Center opened in March 1989 and has been planned for children of all ages (primarily geared to audiences between six and 18 years of age) in the lower level.

Spertus Museum is open 10 a.m. to 5 p.m. Sunday through Thursday; and 10 a.m. to 3 p.m. Friday. An admission is charged, except Friday when admission is free.

CHICAGO BOARD OF TRADE, 141 W. Jackson Ave., is the world's oldest and largest futures and futures-options exchange, dating back to 1848. Two visitors' galleries and a mini-museum, located on the fifth floor, are open to the public. Tours are available 9:30 a.m., 11 a.m., and 12:30 p.m. weekdays. Groups of 10 or more must call 435-3590 for reservations. Admission is free.

CHICAGO MERCANTILE EXCHANGE, 30 S. Wacker Dr., is one of the most diversified exchanges, trading futures, futures-options contracts in physical commodities, foreign currencies, in-

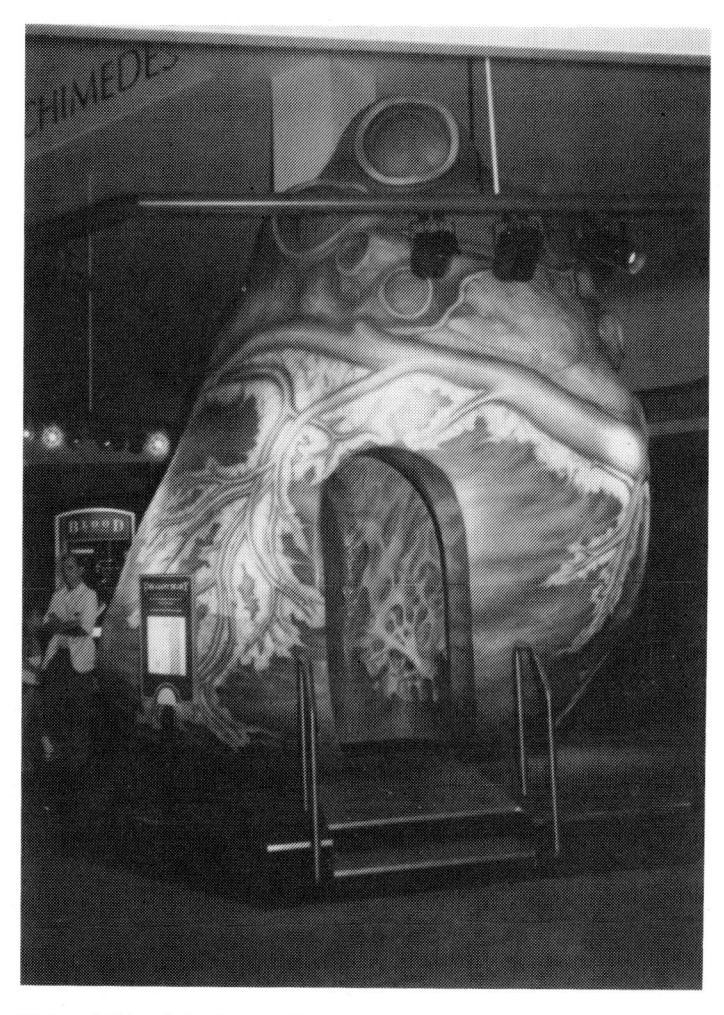

This exhibit of the human heart is displayed at the Museum of Science and Industry. It is one of thousands of exhibits in the museum.

Exhibits in the Museum of Science and Industry.

terest rates, and stock market indices. The visitors' gallery is located on the fourth floor and is open 7:30 a.m. to 3:15 p.m. weekdays. Admission is free.

MUSEUM OF SCIENCE AND INDUSTRY, 57th St. and Lake Shore Dr., is world famous. Founded in 1933 by Sears, Roebuck and Company Chairman **Julius Rosenwald**, the museum today features more than 2,000 exhibits in more than 75 fields. Among its best-known exhibits is the full-scale replica of a southern Illlinois coal mine and the U-505 German submarine captured during World War II.

The museum's Space Center exhibits feature the Apollo 8 spacecraft that was the first to orbit the moon; the lunar module on which the Apollo astronauts trained; the Aurora Mercury spacecraft; and other space artifacts. The center opened in 1986.

The offerings here are diversified and numerous. These range from "The Circus," with its more than 22,000 animated carved figurines, to the "Nobel Hall of Science," honoring America's Nobel laureates in the sciences.

The Museum of Science and Industry is open 9:30 a.m. to 5:30 p.m. daily during the summer; 9:30 a.m. to 4 p.m. weekdays during the winter; and 9:30 a.m. to 5:30 p.m. weekends and holidays the year round. Admission is free.

ROBIE HOUSE, University of Chicago, 5757 Woodlawn Ave., was commissioned by **Frederick C. Robie** in 1908. It was designed by Frank Lloyd Wright and is considered to be one of his greatest architectural achievements. It is perhaps the best example of "Prairie School" Style. Today it houses the Alumni Relations Office of the University of Chicago.

The Robie House is available for tours at noon, Monday through Saturday. Special tours can be arranged by calling the Office of Special Events, 702-8374. An admission is charged.

DUSABLE MUSEUM OF AFRICAN AMERICAN HISTORY, 740 W. 56th Pl., has become one of the nation's most outstanding Afro-American museums. Named in honor of Jean Baptiste Pointe DuSable, the first settler in Chicago, the museum was founded by **Margaret and Charles Burroughs**. Located in Washington Park, the museum features a wide range of memorabilia and artifacts reflecting black American history.

The DuSable Museum is open 9 a.m. to 5 p.m. Monday through Friday and from 1 to 5 p.m. weekends. It is closed on Christmas, New Year's Day, and Easter. An admission is charged.

Chicago Water Tower at night.

Photo by Ron Schramm/Chicago Convention and Visitors Bureau

Designated as a National Historic Landmark in 1963, the Robie House is one of the best-known examples of Frank Lloyd Wright's Prairie House. Prairie Houses are characterized by low, earth-hugging dwellings topped by wide, sweeping roofs. The Robie House is now owned by the University of Chicago and houses the Alumni Association offices. Tours are available Monday through Saturday.

DuSable Museum of African American History Museum is located in Washington Park.

The Polish Museum of America is located in this building at 984 N. Michigan Ave.

CHICAGO ACADEMY OF SCIENCES, 2001 N. Clark St., was founded in 1857, making it the midwest's oldest science museum. It is located in Lincoln Park across the street from the Lincoln Park Zoo. Numerous exhibits are on display on three floors. Among these is a coal forest depicting this area 300 million years ago. There are many of these walk-through exhibits.

The Academy of Sciences is open 10 a.m. to 5 p.m. daily. It is closed on Christmas. An admission is charged, except Mondays when admission is free.

CHICAGO HISTORICAL SOCIETY, Clark St. at North Ave., relates the history of Chicago and Illinois through a large collection of exhibits and materials. It is located in Lincoln Park.

Among some of the historical events presented here include the Abraham Lincoln years and the Great Chicago Fire of 1871 as well as the pioneer days including the Indian story for the area. For those interested in the history of Chicago this museum is a must.

The Chicago Historical Society Museum exhibition galleries are open 9:30 a.m. to 4:30 p.m. Monday through Saturday and 12 noon to 5 p.m. Sunday. It is closed New Year's Day, Thanksgiving, and Christmas. An admission is charged, except Mondays when admission is free.

INTERNATIONAL MUSEUM OF SURGICAL SCIENCES AND HALL OF FAME, International College of Surgeons, 1524 N. Lake Shore Dr., was founded by **Dr. Max Thorek** in 1956. It boasts one of the most extensive medical collections in its 32 exhibit halls. Among its many displays is Napoleon's death mask, a 1920s iron lung, one of Florence Nightingale's nurse's caps, an authentic 1873 apothecary, and the first stethoscope. Also, the Hall of Immortals includes 12 eight-foot sculptures of such early exponents of surgical science as Hippocrates, Louis Pasteur, William Harvey, Marie Curie and Wilhelm Roentgen.

The Museum of Surgical Sciences is open 10 a.m. to 4 p.m. Tuesday through Saturday and 11 a.m. to 5 p.m. Sunday. Admission is free (suggested donation $1).

MUSEUM OF CONTEMPORARY ART, 237 E. Ontario St., was founded in 1967 and is devoted to the art of our time. Presenting the finest and most provocative of the contemporary visual and related arts, MCA exhibitions and collections feature both well-known artists and less familiar artists experimenting with new media and concepts. Daily tours compliment exhibitions and are designed to stimulate an understanding of contem-

Sculptor Tom Czarnopys' Untitled, *affectionately known as the "Bark Man," is one of the popular attractions from the Museum of Contemporary Art's permanent collection.*

The Museum of Contemporary Art presents the finest and most provocative of the contemporary visual and related arts.

porary art.

The Museum of Contemporary Art is open 10 a.m. to 5 p.m. Tuesday through Saturday and 12 noon to 5 p.m. on Sundays. An admission is charged, except Tuesdays when admission is free.

ORIENTAL INSTITUTE OF THE UNIVERSITY OF CHICAGO, 1155 E. 58th St., was founded in 1919 by Egyptologist **James Henry Breasted** and is devoted to the study of civilizations in the ancient Near East. Nearly every significant Near Eastern civilization is represented in the museum's collections, dating from ca. 7000 B.C. to ca. 1000 A.D. A large number of the objects on display here were excavated by the institute's field expeditions to Egypt, Iran, Iraq, and Syria-Palestine. Five galleries are included in the museum—Egyptian, Assyrian, Mesopotamian, Persian, and Syro-Palestinian.

The Oriental Institute is open 10 a.m. to 4 p.m. Tuesday through Saturday and 12 noon to 4 p.m. Sunday. Admission is free.

CHICAGO ARCHITECTURE FOUNDATION, 1800 S. Prairie Ave., has four major areas of activity. These include the ArchiCenter, the John J. Glessner and Henry B. Clarke historic houses, and tours of Chicago's architecture. The ArchiCenter is at 330 S. Dearborn St. and serves as an information center as well

Seated cat with incised necklace, identified with the Goddess Bastet, ca. 664-30 B.C., on exhibit at The Oriental Institute Museum, the University of Chicago.

The exterior of the Oriental Institute building from the northwest.

as changing exhibitions on architecture. The Glessner house, built in 1887, is Architect H. H. Richardson's only surviving design in Chicago. The Clarke house, built in 1836, is in the Greek Revival style and restored by the City of Chicago, which moved it to its present location near the Glessner house. The Clarke house is the oldest surviving house in Chicago. The Foundation also offers over 50 architectural tours of Chicago.

The ArchiCenter is open 9:30 a.m. to 5 p.m. Monday through Friday and 10 a.m. to 4 p.m. Saturday. The Glessner and Clarke houses are open 11 a.m. to 3 p.m. Tuesday through Sunday, April through October, and 11 a.m. to 3 p.m. Tuesday, Thursday, Saturday and Sunday, November through March. Admission to the ArchiCenter is free. An admission is charged for tours of the Glessner and Clarke houses. For information, call 326-1393 (recorded tour information, 782-1776).

BALZEKAS MUSEUM OF LITHUANIAN CULTURE, 6500 S. Pulaski Rd., was founded in 1966 and moved to its present location in 1986. The museum features exhibits dealing with Lithuanian heritage and culture. Included are medieval arms and armor, rare prints, maps, books, coins, paintings and other materials dating back to the time Lithuania was an independent country.

Balzekas Museum is open 10 a.m. to 4 p.m. daily. It is closed Christmas and New Year's Day. An admission is charged.

COPERNICUS CULTURAL AND CIVIC CENTER, 5216 W. Lawrence Ave., serves as the Polish cultural center as well as a civic center for the Northwest section of the city. It was opened in 1981 and among its exhibits are artifacts, books, paintings, and tapestries. The Copernicus Cultural Center's hours vary with special events. The event determines the admission charge. For information call 777-8898.

MEXICAN FINE ARTS CENTER MUSEUM, 1852 W. 19th St., opened its doors in 1987 in Harrison Park and is billed as the largest Latino arts facility in the nation. It features five major exhibits during the year and the focus is on the various components of Mexican art (e.g. contemporary art, folk art). The museum also offers classes.

The Mexican Fine Arts Center Museum is open 10 a.m. to 5 p.m. Tuesday through Sunday. Admission is free. Group tours are conducted in English and/or Spanish. For additional information call 738-1503.

POLISH MUSEUM OF AMERICA, 984 N. Milwaukee Ave.,

The Ukrainian National Museum at 2453 West Chicago Ave.

features objects relating to Polish history, art, and culture. Its collections contain 350 paintings by Polish artists as well as the memorabilia of Thaddeus Kosciusko, Polish patriot, and Ignace Jan Paderewski, noted Polish pianist and statesman. The Polish Museum is open 12 noon to 5 p.m. daily. Admission is free.

VIETNAM MUSEUM, 5002 N. Broadway, was founded by Vietnam veteran Joe Hertel at this location March 5, 1988. It contains three rooms of military and civilian memorabilia from both Free World and NVA/VC Communist forces. Among the displays are uniforms, clothing, photographs, art, souvenirs, letters, military insignias and patches, currency, stamps, and publications. The museum's library contain books, periodicals, photographs, diaries and videos, and is available to students and researchers by appointment. The museum honors all who served in the Vietnam War and is a place where those who were there can come and remember and reflect, and those who were not there can come and learn about a turbulent era in history.

The Vietnam Museum is open 1 to 5 p.m., Tuesday through Friday and 11 a.m. to 5 p.m. weekends. It is closed on Mondays and weekdays during the months of January and February. Admission is free. For further information, call 728-6111.

SWEDISH AMERICAN HISTORICAL SOCIETY, 5125 N. Spaulding Ave., serves as a cultural and research center. It is open weekdays from 8:30 a.m. to 4:30 p.m. and by appointment. It is closed on holidays. Admission is free.

SWEDISH AMERICAN MUSEUM, 5211 N. Clark St., was founded by **Kurt Mathiasson** in 1976. Its collection includes photographs, publications, and artifacts dealing with Swedish American history. It is open 11 a.m. to 4 p.m. Tuesday through Friday, and 11 a.m. to 3 p.m. Saturday. Admission is free.

UKRAINIAN NATIONAL MUSEUM, 2453 W. Chicago Ave., features a collection of folk art, musical instruments, household items, agricultural implements, architectural samples, and other holdings. It is open 12 noon to 3 p.m. Sunday and by appointment other days. An admission is charged.

JANE ADDAMS' HULL HOUSE MUSEUM, University of Illinois Chicago, 800 S. Halsted St., Chicago's first settlement house, founded in 1889 by **Jane Addams** and **Ellen Gates Starr**. The original building was an old mansion built by **Charles J. Hull**. The University has restored two of the original buildings— the Hull Mansion, dating back to 1856, and the Resi-

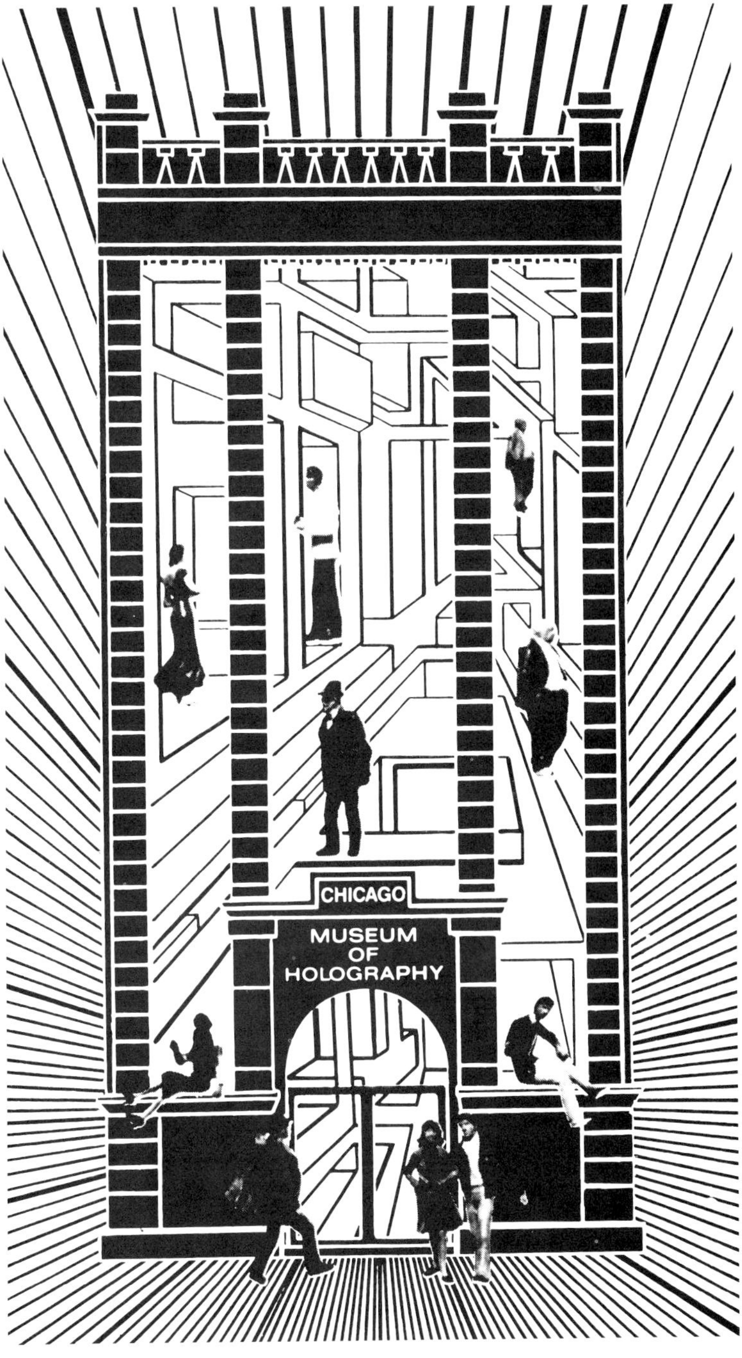
CHICAGO
MUSEUM
OF
HOLOGRAPHY

dents' Dining Hall, opened in 1905. Jane Addams won the Nobel Peace Prize in 1931 for her work for international peace.

The Hull House Museum is open 10 a.m. to 4 p.m. weekdays and 12 noon to 5 p.m. Sunday during the summer and 10 a.m. to 4 p.m. weekdays during the winter. It is closed on holidays. Admission is free.

MORTON B. WEISS MUSEUM OF JUDAICA, K.A.M. Isaiah Israel Congregation, 1100 Hyde Park Blvd., features a collection of religious and cultural artifacts. The museum is housed in the oldest Jewish congregation in the Midwest. Formed in 1847, K.A.M. Isaiah Israel is located in a landmark Byzantine-style sanctuary designed in 1924. It is open 10 a.m. to 4 p.m. weekdays and 10 a.m. to noon Sunday. Admission is free.

MUSEUM OF HOLOGRAPHY, 1134 W. Washington Blvd., was founded in 1976 as part of the Fine Arts Research & Holographic Center, the most complete and comprehensive institution in the world devoted to the display and development of three-dimensional laser images, including a School of Holography and a research facility.

The museum is open to the general public 12:30 to 5 p.m. Wednesday through Sunday. Reserved group tours are conducted Mondays and Tuesdays. An admission is charged.

MUSEUM OF BROADCAST COMMUNICATIONS, 800 S. Wells St. at River City, features a collection of historic radio and television shows, as well as broadcast commercials. Phone 987-1500 for a schedule of screenings and special events. Suggested donations of $3 for adults, $2 for students and $1 for seniors.

PRINTERS ROW PRINTING MUSEUM, 731 S. Plymouth Ct., is housed in an 1897 building in the "Printers Row" district on Chicago's south side. Among the collections are 19th century printing presses still used to print wedding invitations, announcements, and Christmas cards.

The Printing Museum is open 9 a.m. to 5 p.m. Saturday; 10 a.m. to 4 p.m. Sunday. Closed New Year's Day, Mother's Day, Memorial Day, Father's Day, and Christmas. Admission is free. For information, call, 987-1059.

TELEPHONY MUSEUM, 225 W. Randolph St., traces the development of the telephone through 16 exhibit sections. It is operated by Illinois Bell Telephone Company. It is open 8:30 a.m. to 4 p.m. weekdays. Admission is free.

AMERICAN POLICE CENTER AND MUSEUM, 1705-25 S. State St., is the only historical and educational facility pertain-

Exhibits in the American Police Center and Museum.

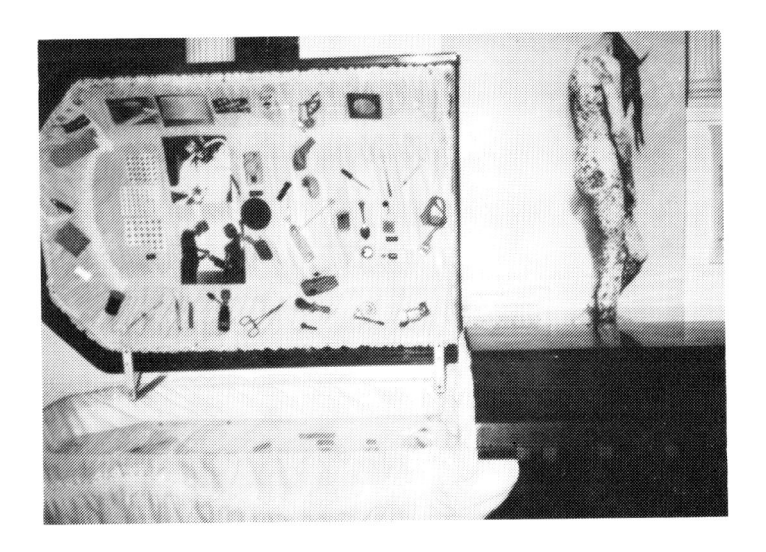

ing to law enforcement that is open to the public in the United States. Exhibits include: the Legacy of Al Capone, the Haymarket Riot of 1886, a memorial room dedicated to police officers killed in the line of duty, and drug abuse and its consequences. Police equipment is displayed as well as artifacts, uniforms, weapons, and photographs. Educational films are also presented.

The Police Center and Museum is open 9 a.m. to 4 p.m. weekdays and by appointment. Admission is charged for adults, children under 12 are admitted free. Special group rates are available for guided tours of 15 or more. For information, call 431-0005.

PEACE MUSEUM, 430 W. Erie St., is the only museum in the country dealing with issues of war and peace. About half of the small museum's exhibitions are traveling exhibits. It is open 12 noon to 5 p.m., Tuesday through Sunday, and 12 noon to 8 p.m. Thursday. Admission is charged.

HISTORIC PULLMAN FOUNDATION, 11111 S. Forrestville Ave., was formed in 1973 to preserve and restore the Pullman area, the company town founded by George M. Pullman's Palace Car Company between 1880-84. The first six families moved into Pullman in January, 1881. By 1886, 14,000 people lived in the railroad town. Prosperity and stability lasted until the Depression of 1893-94 and the Pullman Strike of 1894. In 1898, a year after George Pullman's death, the courts ordered the company to sell its non-industrial real estate. In the years that followed, the community went through several changes. After 1960, when the community was threatened to be destroyed, residents were able to restore the 16-block historic neighborhood, and Pullman was designated a National Historic Landmark.

The Hotel Florence, named for Pullman's daughter, was centerpiece in the community of Pullman. The hotel, opened late in 1881, is undergoing restoration and is now open for tours. It operated until 1975 and offered the only bar permitted in Pullman. One of the features of the restored landmark building is George Pullman's private suite.

The other major landmark is the Greenstone Church, the only church in Pullman. George Pullman hoped the church would be used by all denominations and that the rental would bring a six percent return. This did not occur. Methodists have met at the church since 1914.

The Hotel Florence is open 11 a.m. to 2 p.m. weekdays; 9 a.m. to 3 p.m. Saturday; and 10 a.m. to 3 p.m. Sunday. Guided walking tours leaving from the Pullman Center, 614 E. 113th St., are

The Hotel Florence (top) and the Greenstone Church in historic Pullman, founded by George Pullman in 1880.

scheduled at 12:30 and 1:30 p.m. the first Sunday of each month from May through October. It is closed on holidays. An admission is charged for these guided tours. For tour information, reservations and prices, call 785-8181.

To reach Pullman by car, take I-94 (Calumet/Dan Ryan Expressway) to the 111th Street exit. Proceed west from there. Turn left on Champlain Avenue and continue to 113th Street. The Historic Pullman Center is located one-half block west of Champlain. Illinois Central trains stop at both Pullman (111th Street) and Kensington (115th Street).

Chapter 6
Elsewhere in Cook County

Includes the following communities:

Arlington Heights
Barrington
Bartlett
Berwyn
Blue Island
Buffalo Grove
Des Plaines
Elk Grove Village
Elmwood Park
Evanston
Glencoe
Glenview
Homewood
Kenilworth
La Grange
Lansing
Lemont

Morton Grove
Mount Prospect
Niles
Oak Park
Orland Park
Palatine
River Grove
Riverside
Schaumburg
Skokie
South Holland
Tinley Park
Western Springs
Wheeling
Wilmette
Winnetka

The Museum Listings and Historic Sites
Arlington Heights Historical Museum
Baha'i House of Worship
Barrington History Museum
(Continued on the next Page)

Bartlett Historical Museum
Blue Island Museum
Bradford Museum of Collector's Plates
Cernan Earth and Space Center
Czechoslovak Heritage Museum
Des Plaines Historical Museum
Evanston Historical Society
Farmhouse Museum
Frank Lloyd Wright Home and Studio
Glencoe Historical Museum
Glenview Historical Museum
Grosse Point Lighthouse Park
Hartung's License Plate and Auto Museum
Historical Society of Elmwood Park
Historical Society of Oak Park/River Forest
Homewood Historical Museum
Hostert Log Cabins
Kennilworth Historical Museum
La Grange Historical Museum
Ladd Arboretum and Ecology Center
Landmark Museum/Bremen Historical Society
Lansing Historical Museum
Lemont Historical Museum
Mitchell Indian Museum
Morton Grove Historical Museum
Mount Prospect Historical Museum
Mother Theresa Museum
Niles Historical Museum
Oak Park Conservatory
Palatine Historical Society
Paarlberg Farmstead Homestead
Raupp Memorial Museum
Riverside Historical Museum
Romanian Folk Art Museum
Skokie Historical Society
South Holland Museum
The Grove
Van Oostenbrugge Centennial Home
Western Springs Historical Museum
Wheeling Historical Museum
Wilmette Historical Museum
Winnetka Historical Museum

Chapter 6
Elsewhere in Cook County

This section begins at Oak Park on Chicago's West Side. Oak Park is selected because so much of the city is covered in its historic district. It is only 15 or 20 minutes from Chicago's Loop.

OAK PARK

OAK PARK (pop. 54,887), settled in 1833 and incorporated in 1901, is west on I-290. Its western boundary is Harlem Ave.

The noted author **Ernest Hemingway** was born July 21, 1899 at 439 N. Oak Park Ave., Oak Park. His parents were Clarence Edmonds (Ed) Hemingway, a medical doctor, and Grace Hall Hemingway. He was a colorful character who fought in and reported on wars, hunted big game, married four times and survived several near-fatal accidents. Among some of his most notable works are "The Sun Also Rises" (1926), "A Farewell to Arms" (1929), "For Whom the Bell Tolls" (1940), and "The Old Man and the Sea" (1952), which earned him the 1954 Nobel prize for literature. Hemingway shocked the world when he committed suicide, July 2, 1961.

One of America's most influential and imaginative architects, **Frank Lloyd Wright** (1867-1959) designed more than 150 buildings in his famous Prairie style. Twenty-five of these still remain in Oak Park where he lived and had his studios at the time he was creating this distinctively American design style. He designed his home for his bride when he was only 22 years old. When he and his wife separated in 1909, Wright closed his studio and moved from Oak Park where he had lived for 20 years. It was while he was still at Oak Park that he designed **Unity Temple, Larkin Office Building**, and the **Robie and Coonley Houses**. During his final years, Wright designed two of his most famous projects, the Guggenheim Museum in New York City and the Marin County, California, Civic Center.

The FRANK LLOYD WRIGHT HOME AND STUDIO, at Forest and Chicago Aves., was designated a National Historic Landmark in 1976. It is located along the streets of the Frank Lloyd Wright Prairie School of Architecture National Historic District which features 13 of the buildings he designed, including the first public building, Unity Temple. Tours of the Home and Studio are available at 11 a.m., 1 and 3 p.m. Monday through

The Frank Lloyd Wright Home and Studio in Oak Park.

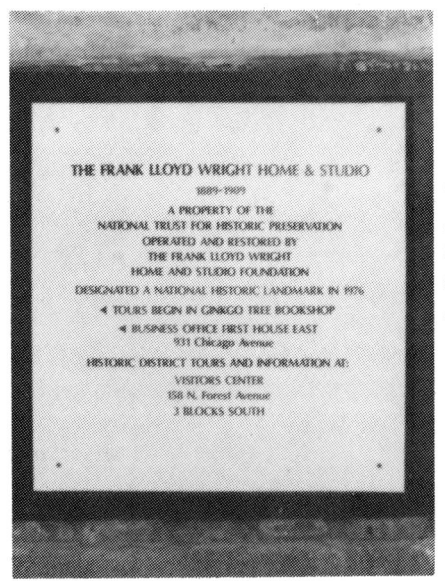

This plaque at the Wright Home provides tour information about this historic site as well as the Oak Park historic district.

The Cernan Earth and Space Center, on the campus of Triton College, is named in honor of Astronaut Eugene A. Cernan. The Navy captain commanded the Apollo 17 mission in December, 1972. In this final mission to the moon, Cernan and Astronaut Harrison Schmitt remained on the moon for 75 hours. He also participated in the Gemini 9 and Apollo 10 missions. Born in Chicago, Cernan grew up in the suburbs and was graduated from Proviso High School in Maywood.

Friday and continuously from 11 a.m. to 4 p.m. on the weekends. A walking tour of the historic district is also available daily. An admission is charged for all tours.

The Ridgeland/Oak Park Historic District is a physical record of Oak Park's development from 1870 to 1920. The District is named for two original communities which grew together to form the present village of Oak Park. There are 31 buildings or blocks of which only two buildings, Unity Temple, 875 Lake St., and the George W. Smith House, 404 Home, were designed by Frank Lloyd Wright. Unity Temple and the Farson-Mills House, 217 Home, designed by George Maher in 1897, are the individual buildings of national significance.

Among the historical attractions in Oak Park are:

HISTORICAL SOCIETY OF OAK PARK AND RIVER FOREST, 217 Home Ave., Oak Park, is housed in the **Farson-Mills House**, the **Pleasant Home**. The house was designed in 1897 for **John Farson** in the style of "Prairie School" architecture by **George W. Maher**, not Frank Lloyd Wright. The Pleasant Home was commissioned by Farson, a prominent banker and philanthropist whose trademark was a red necktie worn for all occasions. Maher designed five houses in Oak Park. Pleasant Home is listed on the National Register of Historic Places. The Museum Room of the Society is open 2 to 4 p.m. Sundays without charge. Tours of the rest of the building are conducted by the Park District of Oak Park from 2 to 3:30 p.m. on weekends. An admission is charged for these tours.

OAK PARK CONSERVATORY, 617 Garfield St., is affiliated with the Oak Park Parks and Recreation Department. It has three distinct and separate display areas—The Desert House, the Tropical House, and the Fern House. It is open 10 a.m. to 4 p.m. daily, except Monday. Admission is free.

ELMWOOD PARK

Northwest of Oak Park is ELMWOOD PARK (pop. 2,117), incorporated in 1914.

HISTORICAL SOCIETY OF ELMWOOD PARK, Elmwood Park Library, 4 Conti Pkwy., exhibits historic photos and publishing artifacts. It is open during library hours.

RIVER GROVE

West of Elmwood Park is RIVER GROVE (pop. 10,368), home of Triton College. River Grove, incorporated in 1888, can be reached off I-90 or I-290 by taking Cumberland Ave.

The CERNAN EARTH AND SPACE CENTER is located on

the campus of Triton College, 2000 5th Ave. Space related historic artifacts and gift shop merchandise can be found here. A 100-seat dome theater provides planetarium shows, Cinema-360 wrap around films, and laser light shows. The Space Center is open 9 a.m. to 5 p.m. Monday, 9 a.m. to 9 p.m. Tuesday through Thursday, 9 a.m. to 10 p.m. Friday and Saturday, and 12 noon to 4 p.m. Sunday. An admission is charged for the theater programs.

BERWYN

Just south of Oak Park is BERWYN (pop. 46,849), founded in 1890 and incorporated in 1891.

The CZECHOSLOVAK HERITAGE MUSEUM, 2701 S. Harlem Ave., focuses on Czech artifacts, cut glass, porcelain, folk costumes, and musical instruments. It is open 10 a.m. to 4 p.m. weekdays.

RIVERSIDE

Just west of Berwyn is RIVERSIDE (pop. 9,236), incorporated in 1875. The village was designed as a model suburb by **Frederick Law Olmsted** and **Calvert Vaux.**

RIVERSIDE HISTORICAL MUSEUM, Longcommon Rd. and Pine Ave., features local history. It is open 10 a.m. to 2 p.m. Saturday or by appointment (4 weeks in advance).

EVANSTON

North of Chicago is EVANSTON (pop. 73,706), settled in 1826; platted in 1854; and incorporated in 1892. It was the home of **Frances E. Willard** (1839-1898) and is site of the national headquarters for the **Woman's Christian Temperance Union.**

Charles Pajeau, an Evanston stonemason, introduced **Tinkertoys** at the 1913 American Toy Fair. It was a year before they caught on but since 1913, more than 100 million Tinkertoy sets have been sold. Newspaper columnist **Drew Pearson** (1897-1969) was born in Evanston. Another celebrity of sorts was Actor **Tom Neal** (1914-72), who was convicted of murdering his third wife, **Gail Evatt**, in 1965.

EVANSTON HISTORICAL SOCIETY, 225 Greenwood St., is housed in the former home of **Charles Gates Dawes** (1865-1951), who served as vice president of the United States from 1925 to 1929 under **President Calvin Coolidge.** Dawes was chairman of the board of the City National Bank & Trust Co. of Chicago from 1932 until his death in 1951. The home was originally built in 1894 for **Robert D. Sheppard.** It became the home of Dawes in 1909. Exhibits focus on local history. The library, dining room, and great hall have been restored to their 1925-29

The former home of Vice President Charles Gates Dawes serves as the museum for the Evanston Historical Society. Dawes, a successful banker, served as vice president under President Coolidge.

ILLINOIS RANKS 24TH IN SIZE

Illinois ranks 24th in size among all the states, and 8th in size among the Midwestern States.

appearance. It is open 1 to 5 p.m. Monday, Tuesday, Thursday, Friday, and Saturday. It is closed on holidays. Admission is charged.

GROSSE POINT LIGHTHOUSE PARK, 2535 Sheridan Rd., is the site of a Visitor/Maritime Center that interprets the Great Lakes heritage. The lighthouse was built in 1873 by the government after a number of shipwrecks off the Lake Michigan shoreline. The promontory, on which the lighthouse stands, was named by early French fur traders in the 17th century. By 1870, over 12,000 ships entered and left the port of Chicago annually, with many passing the shoals off the Evanston point.

Today, the lighthouse is the center of a complex of environmental and cultural activities. The Center for Natural Landscaping is located in the south fog house that was converted into a greenhouse. It contains plants, birds, insects, animals, and minerals native to the area. Grosse Point Lighthouse Park is open weekends, June through September. Admission is charged.

LADD ARBORETUM AND ECOLOGY CENTER, 2024 McCormick Blvd., stretches along the boulevard on a narrow 23-acre strip of reclaimed land along the North Shore Channel. Highlights include the Rotary International Friendship Garden, Cherry Tree Walk, Women's Terrace, bird sanctuary, and prairie restoration area. The arboretum is open all the time. The Ecology Center hours are 9 a.m. to 4:30 p.m. Tuesday through Saturday. Admission is free.

ROMANIAN FOLK ART MUSEUM, 2526 Ridgeway, features the nation's largest collection of Romanian folk art and is housed in the **Rodica and Michael Perciali** home, founders of the museum. Of special interest are the costumes from the 18 regions of Romania. It is open 2 to 5 p.m. Saturday, except holidays. Donations are accepted.

PREHISTORIC LIFE MUSEUM, 704 Main St., features displays of fossils dating back one and a half billon years ago. Also displayed are minerals, crystals, Indian and Eskimo art. It is open 10:30 a.m. to 5:30 p.m. Monday, Tuesday, Thursday and Friday, and 10 a.m. to 5 p.m. Saturday. It is closed Wednesday, Sunday and major holidays. Admission is free.

MITCHELL INDIAN MUSEUM, on the campus of Kendall College, 2408 Orrington Ave., was opened in 1977 to house the American Indian collection of **Betty and John Mitchell** and items from other donors. The collection includes art and artifacts from prehistoric times to the present. It is open 9 a.m. to 4 p.m.

The Grosse Point Lighthouse, in Evanston, serves as an interpretive center for Great Lakes heritage.

Monday through and Friday; 1 to 4 p.m. Sunday. It is closed for the College holidays of Thanksgiving, from Christmas through New Year's Day, and Easter. Donations are appreciated.

WILMETTE

Just north of Evanston is WILMETTE (pop. 28,221), incorporated in 1872. It was named for **Antoine Ouilmette**, a French-Canadian fur trader who settled by the Chicago River in 1790. In 1829, Ouilmette and his part-Indian wife, **Archange**, moved to a cabin near the foot of present-day Lake St. That same year Archange and her children received two square miles of land under the **Treaty of Prairie du Chien**. This land, known as the "Ouilmette Reservation," was east of 15th St. and by 1844 had been sold when the Ouilmette family joined the Indian tribes in Iowa.

WILMETTE HISTORICAL MUSEUM, 565 Hunter Rd., presents the history of the community from pre-Columbian Indians through the present. It is open 9:30 a.m. to noon and 1:30 to 4 p.m. Tuesday, Wednesday, and Thursday; 2 to 5 p.m. weekends. It is also open 7:30 to 9 p.m. the first Monday of each month. It is closed July and August. Admission is free.

BAHA'I HOUSE OF WORSHIP, on Linden Ave. off Sheridan Rd., took more than 40 years to complete and is an architectural marvel as well as a house of worship. The cornerstone was laid in 1912, but actual construction began in 1921. The structure was completed and dedicated in 1953. A visitor's center on the lower level provides information on the Baha'i Faith and the construction of the House of Worship. The Baha'i Faith began in 1844 in what is now Iran. It is an independent world religion and is the most widely spread religion in the world after Christianity. The headquarters of the National Spiritual Assembly of the Baha'is of the United States, the administrative body for the Baha'is of the U.S., is located near the House of Worship. The House of Worship is open 10 a.m. to 10 p.m. daily from May 15 to October 14; 10 a.m. to 5 p.m. daily from October 15 to May 14. Admission is free.

KENILWORTH

KENILWORTH (pop. 2,708), just north of Wilmette, was incorporated in 1896. The town was developed by Joseph Sears and was named for Sir Walter Scott's "Kenilworth." Originally the streets were named for American authors but have been renamed since using names from Sir Walter Scott's "Kenilworth."

KENILWORTH HISTORICAL MUSEUM, 415 Kenilworth Ave., features local history. It is open from 1 to 3 p.m. Monday

The Baha'i House of Worship is located in Wilmette.

and most Sundays from 2 to 4 p.m., and by appointment.
WINNETKA
WINNETKA (pop. 12,772), to the north, was settled in 1836 and incorporated in 1869.

WINNETKA HISTORICAL MUSEUM, 1140 Elm St., is housed in the old Cove School, formerly the Skokie School. The Skokie School was opened in 1922 as one of the nation's first junior high schools. The museum, opened to the public in November, 1988, emphasizes local history. It is open from 1 to 4 p.m. Tuesday, Thursday and Saturday or by special arrangements.
GLENCOE
North of Winnetka is GLENCOE (pop. 9,200), settled in 1836 and incorporated in 1869.

GLENCOE HISTORICAL MUSEUM, 305 Randolph St., focuses on local history. It is open 2 to 4 p.m. the second Sunday of the month, September through April, and the third Sunday in May. Closed during the summer months. Available at the museum are four bike hikes to find historical and architecturally significant structures and buildings in the village.
SKOKIE
Just west of Evanston, north of I-90, off I-94, is SKOKIE (pop. 60,278), originally called Niles Center. The first permanent settlers arrived in 1854 and the village was incorporated as Niles Center in 1888. The name was changed to Skokie in 1940. The Haben House is listed on the National Register of Historic Places. The oldest municipal building is the fire station built in 1887 by the Niles Center Volunteer Fire Department.

SKOKIE HISTORICAL SOCIETY, 8031 Florel Ave., maintains the restored log cabin, built by **Nicholas Meyers**, a Swiss immigrant. It has been furnished in 1840s decor. It is open 2 to 4 p.m. Thursday.
MORTON GROVE
On the west side of I-94, adjacent to Skokie, is MORTON GROVE (pop. 23,747), incorporated in 1895.

MORTON GROVE HISTORICAL MUSEUM, Harrier Park, 6140 Dempster St., is housed in a restored historic house. It is open 2 to 4 p.m. Sunday.
NILES
Just west of Morton Grove is NILES (pop. 30,3630), incorporated in 1899. There are two attractions in Niles.

BRADFORD MUSEUM OF COLLECTOR'S PLATES, 9333 Milwaukee Ave., has the largest permanent collection of limited edition collector's plates. There are over 1300 plates on exhibit. The museum is operated by the Bradford Exchange. It is open 9 a.m. to 4 p.m. weekdays, 10 a.m. to 5 p.m. weekends. An admission is charged on weekdays and Saturday. Admission is free on Sunday.

The NILES HISTORICAL MUSEUM, 8970 Milwaukee Ave., is located in a three-story building, a local landmark, was built in 1923 for Cook County sheriff's quarters. The building is one of the oldest municipal structures in Niles. Among some of the exhibits is an 1886 covered wagon, a c. 1900 bakery wagon as well as 19th century farm implements and tools. The museum opened in the fall of 1986. It is open 10:30 a.m. to 3 p.m. Wednesday and Friday and 2 to 4 p.m. the first and third Sundays, except in July and August. Tours are available upon request. Donations are accepted.

In the western section of Cook County are:

ARLINGTON HEIGHTS

ARLINGTON HEIGHTS (pop. 66,116) was incorporated in 1887. The first settlers arrived in 1841.

ARLINGTON HEIGHTS HISTORICAL MUSEUM, 500 N. Vail (at Fremont), features local history exhibits including three period buildings representing the founding stage of the village (log cabin); the Victorian era (The Muller House); and the early 1900s (The Banta House). Also on display is the Martha Mills Doll Collection. Tours are available from 1 to 4 p.m. Saturday and 2 to 5 p.m. Sunday or through special arrangements made by calling 255-1225. An admission is charged.

BUFFALO GROVE

Just north of Arlington Heights is BUFFALO GROVE (pop. 22,230), incorporated in 1958. The northern section of the village is located in Lake County. The first settlers, German immigrants from the Alsace-Lorraine region, arrived in the mid-1840s. St. Mary's Catholic Church, the village's most prominent landmark, was built by families of the early settlers in 1899.

RAUPP MEMORIAL MUSEUM is owned by the Buffalo Grove Park District and operated by the Buffalo Grove Historical Society. Its collection of artifacts commemorates the American Indians and local history. For information, call 459-5700. Admission is free.

WHEELING

Northeast of Arlington Heights is WHEELING (pop. 23,266), incorporated in 1894. The first settlers, mostly of English stock, arrived in 1833. In 1836, Milwaukee Ave. was designated Post Road between Chicago and Green Bay, which led to development of hotels and taverns to serve travelers.

WHEELING HISTORICAL MUSEUM, 251 N. Wolf Rd., is housed in the original Wheeling Village Hall, originally located at 84 S. Milwaukee Ave. Focus of the museum, through permanent and changing exhibits, is on local history. It is open 1 to 5 p.m. Sunday and 10 a.m. to 1 p.m. Tuesday and Thursday.

PALATINE

West of Arlington Heights is PALATINE (pop. 32,166), founded in 1855 and incorporated in 1869.

PALATINE HISTORICAL SOCIETY operates a 1872 Victorian house museum at 224 E. Palatine Rd. It is furnished in the 1870 period. The library features local history. It is open 10 a.m. to 3 p.m. Tuesday and 1:30 to 4:30 p.m. Thursday and Sunday. Admission is free.

MOUNT PROSPECT

South of Arlington Heights is MOUNT PROSPECT (pop. 52,634), founded in 1871 and incorporated in 1917. A contractor named the town for its elevation and prospects of development.

Screen and TV actor **Bruce Boxleitner**, a native of Crystal Lake, Ill., graduated from Mount Prospect High School in 1968. He has starred in several motion pictures and TV series.

MOUNT PROSPECT HISTORICAL MUSEUM, 1100 S. Linneman Rd., features local history. A major exhibit is a cutaway of a 1901 school room. It is open 10 a.m. to 4 p.m. Tuesday through Thursday and 12 noon to 4 p.m. Saturday.

ELK GROVE VILLAGE

South of Mount Prospect is ELK GROVE VILLAGE (pop. 28,679), founded in 1860 and incorporated in 1956. The Elk Grove Historical Society was founded in 1975 under the auspices of the Elk Grove Park District.

The **Henry Schuette** farmhouse at Clearmont and Arlington Heights Rd., dating back to 1856, was donated to the Society and today is operated as the FARMHOUSE MUSEUM, 399 Biesterfield Rd. It has been refurbished and furnished with artifacts of the period. The grounds include several outbuildings and period farm machinery. It is open 2 to 4 p.m. Sunday and by appointment. An admission is charged.

DES PLAINES

East of Mount Prospect is DES PLAINES (pop. 55,374), founded in the 1830s and incorporated in 1925.

Des Plaines Historical Society Museum at Prairie Ave. and Pearson St.

ILLINOIS IS 21ST STATE
Illinois gained statehood, December 3, 1818, the 21st state.

Elk Grove Historical Society operates the Farmhouse Museum, housed in an 1856 farm residence.

THE ILLINOIS STATE MOTTO
The Illinois State motto is *State Sovereignty, National Unity.*

The Mount Prospect Historical Society Museum is located at 1100 S. Linneman Rd.

This is home of the Bartlett Historical Museum at 240 S. Main St.

DES PLAINES HISTORICAL MUSEUM, 789 Pearson, centers on local history. It is open 9 a.m. to 4 p.m. Monday through Friday. It is closed on all national holidays.

ROSEMONT

South of DesPlaines is ROSEMONT (pop. 4,137) founded by Donald E. Stephens, who has served as mayor of the village since 1956.

The DONALD E. STEPHENS MUSEUM OF HUMMEL AND EUROPEAN FOLK ART, in the South Lobby of the Rosemont/O'Hare Exposition Center, 5555 N. River Rd., features the I. M. Hummel figurine collection of Mr. Stephens. Also included are collections of ANRI woodcarvings, Lladro and other European folk art. The museum is open 9 a.m. to 5 p.m. weekdays and 10 a.m. to 2 p.m. Saturdays. Admission and parking are free. For information, call 692-4000.

BARRINGTON

In the far western part of Cook County is BARRINGTON (pop. 9,029), founded in 1850 and incorporated in 1865.

BARRINGTON HISTORY MUSEUM, 212 W. Main St., opened late in the spring of 1989 in the first of three buildings exhibiting and interpreting artifacts, furniture and memorabilia of the Barrington area. The **Applebee House** contains six period rooms depicting the domestic life of a Barrington family between c. 1889, and c. 1925. The museum gift shop is located at 218 W. Main St. in the 1897 Donlea/Kincaid House. Future buildings will include a historic barn, exhibiting the agricultural and horse history of the Barrington area, and a Museum/Archival Research Center. Group tours can be arranged by appointment by calling 381-1730. An admission is charged. The gift shop is open 10 a.m. to 4 p.m. Tuesday through Friday and 10 a.m. to 1 p.m. Saturdays.

The **Octagon House**, 223 W. Main St., is an outstanding surviving example of a fad for octagonal architecture which had its zenith in the 1850s. It is listed on the National Register of Historic Places.

SCHAUMBURG

SCHAUMBURG (pop. 53,355) was founded as Sarah's Grove in 1835 by **Trumball Kent**, a Yankee from Oswego, N.Y. Among the early settlers was **Horace Williams**, founder of Northwestern University. In 1851, the name was changed to Schaumburg in honor of Schaumburg Lippe district of northwest Germany, the former home of many of the immigrant settlers. It remained a

The Merkle Cabin Historical Museum is located in the Spring Valley Nature Sanctuary, 1111 E. Schaumburg Rd., Schaumburg. The sanctuary, operated by the Schaumburg Park District, is listed as a living museum. The Merkle Cabin is open 12 to 3 p.m. weekends; the living museum, 8 a.m. to 5 p.m. daily. The grounds are open from 8 a.m. to sunset daily.

THE ILLINOIS STATE SONG

The Illinois State song is *Illinois*. The words are by Charles H. Chamberlin; sung to the tune of *Baby Mine* by Archibald Johnston.

The Kincaid House, 218 W. Main St., (top) houses the Barrington Area Historical Society Museum. Barrington's Octagon House, 223 W. Main St., (below) is on the National Register of Historic Places.

small farm settlement until the mid-twentieth century when it was finally incorporated in 1956 and consisted of two square miles with a population of 130. The first large residential subdivision began to emerge in 1959.

Robert O. Atcher, star of the old time radio and TV "Barn Dance" on *WGN*, became Schaumburg's second village president in 1959 and is credited with establishing the city as a major corporate area. Today, the village encompasses more than 18 square miles.

BARTLETT

In the southwest corner of the county and spilling over into DuPage County is BARTLETT (pop. 16,792), incorporated in 1891, 18 years after the Chicago & Pacific Railroad began service to the area. The village was named for **Luther Bartlett**, a native of Conway, Mass., who arrived in 1844. He provided the right-of-way and station site for the railroad in 1873.

BARTLETT HISTORICAL MUSEUM, 240 S. Main St., features local and state history exhibits. It is open 12 noon to 3 p.m. the 1st and 3rd Sundays of the month, except July, December and holidays. Admission is free.

GLENVIEW

Off I-294, north of I-90, is GLENVIEW (pop. 33,131), home of Glenview Naval Air Station. The town was incorporated in 1899.

The air strip established for Naval Reserve Aviation at Great Lakes Naval Training Center in 1929 became inadequate by 1936. Approval for The Naval Reserve Aviation base to be moved to the Curtiss-Reynolds airport in Glenview was approved and construction began January 4, 1937. The station was moved to Glenview, May 15, 1937, with **Lt. G. A. T. Washburn**, as commanding officer. The formal commissioning of the base was held August 28, 1937. Glenview was redesignated a "Naval Air Station" on New Year's Day, 1943. Early in World War II, the base was used for primary flight training and was designated as the Primary Training Command. A Carrier Qualifications Training Program was also instituted. Nearly 9,000 aviation cadets received their primary flight training at Glenview. Another 15,000 Navy and Marine Corps pilots were qualified in carrier landings during the war.

One of the flight instructors at Glenview during World War II was movie actor, **Robert Taylor**, a lieutenant. While on duty at the Naval Air Station, he lived with his actress wife, **Barbara Stanwyck**, on North Prospect Avenue in Park Ridge.

In 1946, Glenview Naval Air Station became the Reserve Training Command, home of the Naval Air Reserve Training Command Headquarters.

GLENVIEW HISTORICAL MUSEUM, 1121 Waukegan Rd., focuses on local history. It is open 2 to 5 p.m. Sunday and by appointment.

THE GROVE, 1421 Milwaukee Ave., is a national historic landmark. This facility of the Glenview Park District is listed on the National Register of Historic Places. The 1856 Robert Kennicott house is the center of The Grove's history interpretation programs. The house and grounds have be restored and appear substantially as they did in 1856. They serve as a "living museum." Other buildings in this complex are the Redfield Center, the Interpretive Center, the Grove School House, and Kennicott's original log cabin.

The Grove is open to the public 8 a.m. to 4:30 p.m. weekdays, and 9 a.m. to 5 p.m. on weekends. The Kennicott House is open 1 to 4 p.m. Sundays. It is closed on Christmas Day and New Year's Day. For information, call 299-6096.

HARTUNG'S LICENSE PLATE AND AUTO MUSEUM, 3623 West Lake St., has more than 100 antique automobiles, trucks, tractors, and motorcycles as well as other auto-related collections. Among these is a first issue collection of license plates from every state as well as collections of radiator nameplates, antique hub caps, auto mascots, and other items. Also displayed are toys, bicycles, clocks, watch fobs, and police badges and stars. It is open by appointment by calling 724-4354. Donations are accepted.

WESTERN SPRINGS

On the South Side, off I-294, is WESTERN SPRINGS (pop. 12,876), incorporated in 1886.

The WESTERN SPRINGS HISTORICAL SOCIETY MUSEUM, The Tower, Village Green Hillgrove Ave., is housed in the 112-1/2-foot-high stone Water Tower, built in 1892. It concentrates on local history and is open 10 a.m. to 2 p.m. Saturdays the year-round and 7 to 9 p.m. Thursdays in the summer. The archives, located in Grand Avenue School, is open 9 a.m. to 12 noon Tuesdays.

LA GRANGE

Just east of Western Springs is LA GRANGE (pop. 15,693), settled in the 1830s and incorporated in 1879.

LA GRANGE HISTORICAL MUSEUM, 444 S. La Grange

This is home of the Glenview Historical Museum.

Western Springs Historical Society museum.

Rd., features exhibits and displays centering on local history. It is open 9 a.m. to 12 noon Wednesday.

BLUE ISLAND

BLUE ISLAND (pop. 21,855) was founded in 1835 and incorporated as a village in 1871. Despite the Pullman Strike of 1894 and a devastating fire in 1896, Blue Island served as a major industrial and trade center for southern Cook County.

The site of Blue Island's "Big Fire of May 18, 1896" was the southwest corner of Grove St. and Western Ave. The fire, of mysterious origin, destroyed 26 stores and homes and badly damaged others.

The **Wadhams/Young House**, 2445 W. High St., is listed on the National Register of Historic Places.

John S. Kaufmann, the man who built the **William D. Henke House**, 12939 S. Greenwood Ave., in 1882, was at the Ford Theatre, in Washington, the night **Abraham Lincoln** was shot. In the confusion that followed, every man who resembled the assassin was rounded up and arrested by the police. Kaufmann was one of these men. He was, of course, later released.

The Blue Island Historical Society has prepared a historic tour listing 59 sites. For copies, contact the library.

A 1200 square foot exhibit area, the BLUE ISLAND MUSEUM, is located in the lower level of the Blue Island Public Library, 2433 York St. More than 50 exhibits highlight the more than 150 year history of the community. It is open 9 a.m. to 9 p.m. weekdays and 9 a.m. to 5 p.m. Saturday. It is closed Sunday and holidays.

SOUTH HOLLAND

SOUTH HOLLAND (pop. 24,977) is just north of I-294 and just west of I-94. It was settled by the Dutch in 1846 and incorporated in 1894. There are three historical attractions in South Holland.

These include the PAARLBERG FARMSTEAD HOMESTEAD, 172nd Pl. and Paxton Ave.; the SOUTH HOLLAND MUSEUM, 16250 Wausau Ave.; and the VAN OOSTENBRUGGE CENTENNIAL HOME, 444 E. 157th St.

The Paarlberg Homestead includes a historical farm house and barn and other out buildings built by Dutch pioneers. It is open 1 to 4 p.m. Saturday, May through October. An admission is charged.

The museum focuses on local history and is open 1 to 4 p.m Saturday the year-round. An admission is charged.

The Van Oostenbrugge Home was built in 1858 by Jan Van Oostenbrugge, who had emigrated from the Netherlands. It is open 1 to 4 p.m. Saturdays, May through October. An admission is charged.

HOMEWOOD

Southwest of South Holland is HOMEWOOD (pop. 19,724), platted in 1852 and incorporated in 1893.

It is home of the HOMEWOOD HISTORICAL MUSEUM, 2020 Chestnut Rd. Featuring local history, the museum is open 1 to 3 p.m. Tuesday and Saturday and by appointment.

LANSING

LANSING (pop.29,039) is south of I-80 and I-94 near the Illinois-Indiana state line. It was founded in the 1860s and incorporated in 1893.

LANSING HISTORICAL MUSEUM, 2750 Indiana Ave., features special exhibits and oral history relating to the area. A popular annual exhibit is the "Holidays and Christmas Trees from Many Lands," displayed from Thanksgiving through the first week in January. It is open 6 to 8 p.m. Monday, 10 to 12 noon Wednesday, and 2 to 4 p.m. Saturday, except during June, July and August.

LEMONT

In the far southwest corner of Cook County is LEMONT (pop. 5,640), incorporated in 1873.

The LEMONT HISTORICAL MUSEUM, 306 Lemont St., focuses on local history. It is open 1 to 4 p.m. Sunday.

MOTHER THERESA MUSEUM, 1250 Main St., is dedicated to Mother Theresa, who founded the Franciscan Sisters of Chicago. It is housed in an 1868 structure that is a reproduction of an English mansion. It features memorabilia of Mother Theresa's life. It is open 2 to 5 p.m. Sundays and holidays and at other times by appointment. For information, call 257-2905. Admission is free.

TINLEY PARK

Just off I-80, in the southernmost part of Cook County, is TINLEY PARK (pop. 26,1780), incorporated in 1892.

The LANDMARK MUSEUM OF THE BREMEN HISTORICAL SOCIETY OF TINLEY PARK, 6727 W. 174th St., contains permanent exhibits of Tinley Park/New Bremen history, Indian (particularly the Pottawatomi) exhibits and books, and artifacts from the Wanamacher/Menke archaeological site in Tinley Park. There are changing exhibits of local history. There is a small library for use on the premises, and a research clipping file. The museum is located in a former church, built in 1884. It is open 9 a.m. to 5 p.m. Mondays (except holidays) and (in 1989) certain Saturdays. For information, call 429-4210. An admission is charged.

ORLAND PARK

Just north of Tinley Park is ORLAND PARK (pop. 25,738), incorporated in 1892.

The JACOB HOSTERT LOG CABIN and the BERNARD HOSTERT LOG CABIN are located at West Ave. and 147th St. They are open 2 to 4 p.m. Sundays during the summer months and by appointment. They are located in a wooded area with picnic tables. Admission is free.

THE ILLINOIS STATE BIRD
The Illinois State bird is the Cardinal.

Chapter 7
Touring DuPage County

Includes the following communities:
Addison
Bensenville
Bloomingdale
Carol Stream
Downers Grove
Elmhurst
Glen Ellyn
Hinsdale
Itasca
Lisle
Lombard
Naperville
Oak Brook
Roselle
Villa Park
Warrenville
Wayne
West Chicago
Wheaton
Winfield
Wood Dale

The Museum Listings and Historical Sites

Bensenville Historical Society
Billy Graham Center Museum
Bloomingdale Park District Museum
Cantigny
Colvin House
Cosley Animal Farm and Museum
Downers Grove Historical Museum
DuPage County Historical Museum
DuPage Heritage Gallery
Dunham Castle
Elmhurst Historical Museum
1st Division Museum
Gretna Station Museum/Caboose
Hedges Station
Historical Museum of Addison
Itasca Historical Museum
Jurica Natural History Museum
Kruse House Museum
Lilacia Park
Lisle Depot Museum
Lizzardo Museum of Lapidiary Art
Morton Arboreteum
Naper Settlement
Old Graue Mill and Museum
Perry Mastodon
Robert Crown Center for Health Education
Robert R. McCormick Museum
Stacy's Tavern
Villa Park Historical Society Museum
Warrenville Historical Society
West Chicago Historical Museum
Willowbrook Wildlife Haven
Wood Dale Historical Society

Chapter 7
Touring DuPage County

The creation of DuPage County was accomplished in a two year period that began in early 1837 and ended February 9, 1839, under the leadership of **Capt. Joseph Naper**, who had founded Naperville in the southwest corner of the county in 1831. The new county was formed from the nine southwestern townships of Cook County.

Several national and international leaders with roots in DuPage county are presented and honored in the the not-for-profit DUPAGE HERITAGE GALLERY, in the DuPage Center Atrium, 421 N. County Farm Rd., Wheaton. It is an unusual "museum" in its own right.

Those personalities that have been honored through 1988 include the legendary **Harold "Red" Grange**, gridiron great; **Judge Elbert Gary**, who organized United States Steel; **John "Bet-A-Million" Gates**, founder of Texaco Oil Company; **Col. Robert McCormick**, colorful publisher of the *Chicago Tribune*; **Rev. Billy Graham**, internationally known evangelist; **Everett Mitchell**, an early radio pioneer, credited with many firsts in Chicago broadcasting; **Dr. Kenneth Taylor**, who spent 16 years single handedly converting 66 books of the Bible into modern style and language; **Grote Reber**, who developed the first radio telescope; and **Sherrill Milnes**, one of the world's foremost baritones.

There have been many interesting and famous personalities connected with Wheaton. Among these was **John Wesley Powell** (1834-1902) who arrived here as a youngster. After service in the Union Army, where he lost an arm, Powell became involved in several scientific and geological expeditions in the West. He later became director of the Bureau of Ethnology and the United States Geological Survey.

Edwin Powell Hubble (1889-1953), one of the greatest astronomers of our time, grew up in Wheaton and attended Wheaton schools. He was a brilliant scholar and outstanding athlete and won a scholarship to the University of Chicago. Hubble discovered that our universe was not limited to the Milky Way but extended on to infinity and included thousands of galaxies like our own. He also discovered that the various galaxies were all

The DuPage Heritage Gallery is located in the DuPage County Government Center in Wheaton.

JOHN GATES

COL. ROBERT MCCORMICK

RED GRANGE

REV. BILLY GRAHAM

Among DuPage County "Greats"

Among DuPage County "greats," who at one time resided in the Wheaton area, honored by the DuPage Heritage Gallery include (top, l. to r.) John "Bet-A-Million" Gates, who founded the Texaco Oil Co.; Col. Robert R. McCormick, editor and publisher of the Chicago Tribune and adventurer; (bottom, l. to r.) Harold "Red" Grange, the Wheaton Ice Man, whose exploits on the gridiron raised professional football from a sandlot game to a new national sport; and Rev. Billy Graham, the internationally famous evangelist.

JUDGE ELBERT GARY

DR. KENNETH TAYLOR

GROTE REBER

EVERETT MITCHELL

"Greats" Made Varied Contributions

Others who have been inducted into the DuPage Heritage Gallery are (top, l. to. r.) Judge Elbert H. Gary, who founded United States Steel Corporation, the nation's first billion dollar enterprise; Dr. Kenneth Taylor, translator of the Living Bible; (bottom, l. to r.) Grote Reber, the first radio astronomer; and Everett Mitchell, pioneer radio and TV broadcaster.

receding from our own and that the galaxies farthest away were receding at the greatest speed. He found a mathematical relationship between a galaxy's speed and its distance from Earth. That relationship, called **Hubble's Constant**, has enabled scientists to calculate the approximate size and age of the entire universe.

WHEATON

WHEATON (pop. 43,043) is the county seat of DuPage county. It can be reached off I-88 by taking IL 59 to IL 38 or by taking IL 38 (Roosevelt Rd.) west from I-290. It was settled in the 1830s, platted in 1853, and incorporated in 1859.

Wheaton became the county seat as a result of an election held in 1867, but only after violence that claimed at least one life. Violence occurred at the Wheaton railroad station where Marriot Mott was killed by a rock thrown by an unknown assailant. In all of the changes of county seats in Illinois, this one in DuPage was the only one that resulted in rioting and violence.

The *U.S.S. Wheaton*, a World War I transport ship named for the City of Wheaton, was assigned to bring back the bodies of servicemen for burial after the war. It was on the deck of the *U.S.S. Wheaton* that **President Warren G. Harding** stood when he selected three unmarked caskets to represent the three branches of service in the memorial to the Unknown Soldier in the Arlington National Cemetery.

A major historical attraction in the Wheaton area:

CANTIGNY, two miles west of Wheaton on Winfield Rd., off Roosevelt Rd., is the name of the late Col. Robert R. McCormick's 425-acre estate which today includes two museums. The estate was initially established as Red Oak Farm by **Joseph Medill**, McCormick's grandfather, early-day editor and publisher of the *Chicago Tribune*. McCormick was a long-time editor and publisher of the newspaper. The Robert R. McCormick Museum is housed in the Georgian mansion that was the McCormick home. The mansion is furnished in period pieces. Of particular interest are the dining room, den and weapons room. The tomb of McCormick and his wife is located behind the mansion. At the head of the two floor-level slabs are the life-like figures of McCormick's two dogs. The 1st Division Museum, located in a building on the site of the old stables, relates the story of this Army division, the "Big Red One," particularly during World War I, World War II, and Vietman. McCormick served as a deputy commander of an artillery battalion in the division in

"Cantigny" is the name of the 500-acre country estate of the late Col. Robert R. McCormick, publisher of the Chicago Tribune. This was McCormick's home at "Cantigny."

Colonel McCormick and his first wife, Amy, are buried in the gardens of "Cantigny."

The 1st (The Big Red One) Division Museum is located on the grounds of "Cantigny." McCormick served as an officer in the division during World War I.

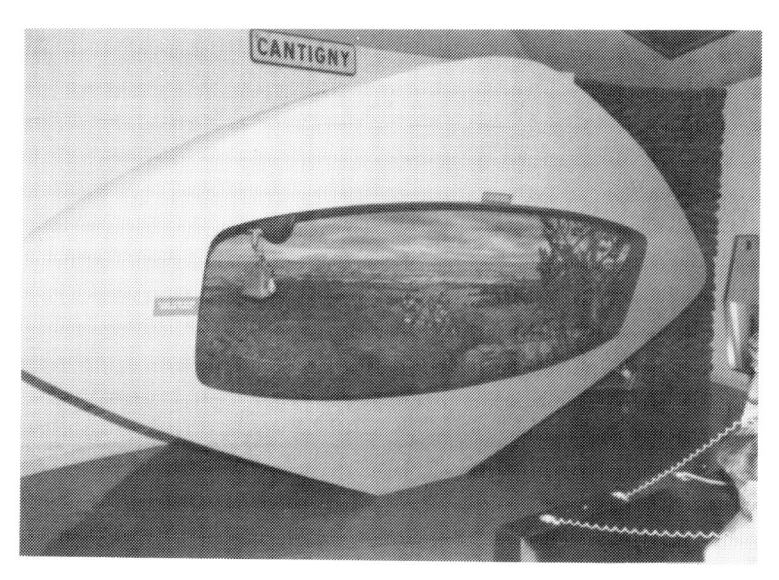

One of the exhibits in the 1st Division Museum at "Cantigny."

World War I. Upon returning home from overseas, he renamed his estate Cantigny, a small French village that was site of the Army's first offensive in Europe.

The McCormick Museum is open 10 a.m. to 5 p.m. daily during the summer months; 10 a.m. to 4 p.m. Tuesday through Sunday during the winter months. It is closed during January. The 1st Army Museum is open 10 a.m. to 5 p.m. daily during the summer; 10 a.m. to 4 p.m. Tuesday through Sunday during the winter. The gardens and grounds are open daily until dusk. It is closed New Year's Day, Thanksgiving and Christmas. Admission is free.

Historical attractions in Wheaton include:

DUPAGE COUNTY HISTORICAL MUSEUM, 102 E. Wesley St., provides a look at the county's past from settlement to present through a variety of exhibits and displays. Collections include costume, coverlets/quilts, toys, farm equipment, household, medical and military objects. Slide programs are available. It is open 10 a.m. to 4 p.m. Monday, Wednesday, Friday and Saturday. Admission is free.

BILLY GRAHAM CENTER MUSEUM, 500 E. Seminary Ave., Wheaton College, contains in-depth presentations on evangelism, offering a visual history of its growth in the United States. The Evangelism in America Hall particularly traces evangelism and revival in America from the early 17th century to the present through a collection of displays, dioramas, and actual artifacts.

The Billy Graham Center Museum is open 9:30 a.m. to 5:30 p.m. Monday through Saturday, and from 1 to 5 p.m. Sunday. An admission is charged.

THE PERRY MASTODON is displayed in the Edwin F. Deicke Exhibit Hall in the Armerding Science Building on the Wheaton College campus. The mastodon remains were discovered in 1963 on the property of **Judge Joseph Sam Perry** in Glen Ellyn. The 16-foot long, nine foot tall mastodon has been reconstructed to show the skeleton on the animal's left side, and a realistically reproduced body covered with shaggy brown hair on the right side. The mastodon that once roamed most of North America some 12,000 years ago became extinct about 8,000 years ago. The Perry mastodon is believed to have suffered a broken leg and died in a deep pool in the east branch of the DuPage River about 11,000 years ago.

The rotating display and audio recorded story can be operated any time between 9 a.m. and 9 p.m. daily. Admission is free.

The Billy Graham Center Museum is located on the campus of Wheaton College.

The Perry Mastodon, found in Glen Ellyn, is exhibited at Wheaton College today.

DuPage County Historical Museum is located in downtown Wheaton.

THE COLVIN HOUSE, 606 N. Main St., is owned by the Wheaton Historic Preservation Council. The house, c. 1887, is a historical and architectural resource center. It is open 10 a.m. to 12 noon Tuesday and 1 to 3 p.m. Saturday. Admission is free.

COSLEY ANIMAL FARM AND MUSEUM, 1356 Gary Ave., includes a pre-1880 barn, old train station, railroad caboose and railway equipment. Visitors can pet and feed the domesticated farm animals and wildlife in a natural setting. It is open 9 a.m. to 4 p.m. Monday through Thursday, and 10 a.m. to 6 p.m. Friday and weekends April through December. Donations are accepted.

The communities on IL 38, from east to west, include Elmhurst (pop. 44,276), Villa Park (pop. 23,155), Lombard (pop. 38,879), Glen Ellyn (pop. 22,743), Wheaton, and West Chicago (pop. 12,550).

ELMHURST

ELMHURST, once known as Cottage Hill, was settled in 1843 and incorporated in 1910. One of its citizens, **Charles P. Bryan**, was a prominent state legislator (1890-98). Later he was appointed ambassador to Japan. His father, **Thomas Barber Bryan** was a prominent Elmhurst resident from the late 1850s until his death. Thomas Bryan served as vice president of the Columbian Exposition in 1893.

The ELMHURST HISTORICAL MUSEUM, 120 E. Park Ave., is housed in the 1892 mansion built for **Village President Henry Glos**. The exhibits and displays provide the history of the building and the community. It is open Tuesday, Thursday, and weekends and by appointment. Call 833-1457 for hours. Admission is free.

LIZZARDO MUSEUM OF LAPIDARY ART, 220 Cottage Hill Ave., features a display of minerals, gems, oriental jade and intricate objects created from gems and ivory. It is open 10 a.m. to 5 p.m. Tuesday through Saturday, and 1 to 5 p.m. Sunday. It is closed New Year's Day, Easter, July 4th, Thanksgiving, and Christmas. An admission is charged. Friday is a free day.

VILLA PARK

VILLA PARK was incorporated in 1914.

VILLA PARK HISTORICAL SOCIETY MUSEUM, 220 S. Villa Ave., is located in the Villa Avenue Station on the Chicago, Aurora & Elgin line. In addition to several railroad exhibits the museum features local history of Villa Park. It is open 9 a.m. to noon Saturday and 9 a.m. to 4 p.m. on Sunday.

The Ardmore Avenue Station on the C. A. & E. line was built

The Elmhurst Historical Museum is located in this 1892 limestone mansion built for Henry and Lucy Glos.

in 1910 and served commuters until 1957. It has been placed on the National Register of Historic Places. The **Ovaltine Company** built its original plant on S. Villa Ave. in 1917. This has been the only place in the U.S.A. where the popular drink was manufactured.

LOMBARD

LOMBARD was settled in 1834 and incorporated in 1869. An unusual attraction here is Lilacia Park, an eight-and-a-half acre botanical garden. An 1888 coach house is also located here. The park is open 9 a.m. to 9 p.m. daily.

The museum, operated by the Lombard Historical Society, is open 1 to 4 p.m. Sunday through Wednesday and by appointment. It features local history. Admission is charged.

GLEN ELLYN

GLEN ELLYN was platted in 1851 and incorporated in 1892. It had several names until 1874, when it became Prospect Park. This village became Glen Ellyn in 1891. The mastodon on display at Wheaton College was discovered on the Judge Joseph Sam Perry property in Glen Ellyn on October 16, 1963.

STACY'S TAVERN, Main St. and Geneva Rd., was built by **Moses Stacy**, in 1846 as a home for his family and an inn for travelers along the St. Charles Road route to and from Chicago. The inn operated until 1892. The old inn is listed on the National Register of Historic Places. It is open 1:30 to 4:30 p.m. Wednesday and Sunday. It is closed New Year's Day, Easter, Thanksgiving, and Christmas. An admission is charged.

Another special attraction in Glen Ellyn is the WILLOWBROOK WILDLIFE HAVEN in the Willowbrook Forest Preserve, Park Blvd. between Roosevelt and Butterfield Rds. It is open from 9 a.m. to 5 p.m. daily. It is closed Thanksgiving, Christmas, and New Year's Day. Admission is free.

CAROL STREAM

Adjacent to Wheaton is CAROL STREAM (pop. 27,000).

The GRETNA STATION MUSEUM/CABOOSE 543 MUSEUM are located in Armstrong Park, 391 Illini Dr., and feature local and railroad history. The museums are open 1 to 3 p.m. the third Sunday of each month, April through November and by appointment. Admission is free.

WINFIELD

West of Wheaton is WINFIELD (pop. 4,745), incorporated in 1921.

HEDGES STATION, Winfield Rd., is the oldest remaining

Historic Stacy Tavern is located on Geneva Rd. in Glen Ellyn.

railroad depot in the state. It was built by an entrepreneur named **John Hedges** in 1849 and served as a depot for the Galena and Chicago Union Railroad. Over the years the building has been used for a number of purposes. It is open to the public by appointment only. For information call 653-1489.

WEST CHICAGO

WEST CHICAGO was incorporated in 1906 and is located west of Winfield and Wheaton. The historical attractions here:

KRUSE HOUSE MUSEUM, 527 Main St., is housed in the 1916 home of the Kruse family, who were railroaders. It features 1920 era household items. It is open 12 noon to 3 p.m. Saturday, and 1 to 3 p.m. Sunday, May through September. Admission is free.

WEST CHICAGO HISTORICAL MUSEUM, 132 Main St., is housed in the 1884 former Town Hall and Fire Station and the 1890 Chicago, Burlington and Quincy Railroad Station. Among the museum's collections are railroad memorabilia and equipment, tools and farm implements. It is open 11 a.m. to 3 p.m. Thursday through Saturday. Admission is free.

Interstate 88, formerly I-5, runs across the southern part of the county. This runs through Illinois' "high tech corridor." The communities along this route, from east to west, include Oak Brook, Hinsdale, Downers Grove, Woodridge, Lisle, Naperville, and Warrenville.

OAK BROOK

OAK BROOK (pop. 7,263) began as Fullersburg, for its founder Benjamin Fuller in 1840. Fullersburg, located in and between today's Oak Brook and Hinsdale, became a thriving community but declined soon after the railroad was completed through Hinsdale in the 1860s. In 1898, **Frank O. Butler** purchased land and a summer home on 31st St. along Salt Creek and named it Oak Brook. Ted Mohlman became Oak Brook's first Village president in 1946. Equestrian events in the 1959 Pan American games were held here. Oak Brook was once the site of one of the largest Pottawatomi Indian villages, called Sauganakka, between the late 1600s and 1833.

Oak Brook is home of the OLD GRAUE MILL AND MUSEUM, York and Spring Rds. The mill was constructed in 1852 by **Fred Graue**. It is still operational and is the only operating waterwheel gristmill in Illinois. The mill served as one of the Underground Railway stations in Illinois that assisted slaves in making their way north and to freedom before the Civil War.

The Old Graue Mill and Museum in Oak Brook. The mill, on Salt Creek, was built in 1852 by Fred Graue.

The ground floor of the museum features Civil War relics. The upper two floors contain exhibits covering the 1840-85 period. Weavers and spinners put on demonstrations daily. It has been designated as a National Historic Landmark and as a Mechanical Engineering Landmark.

The Old Graue Mill and Museum is open from 10 a.m. to 5 p.m. daily from mid-May through mid-November. An admission is charged.

HINSDALE

South of Oak Brook is HINSDALE (pop. 16,726) originally called Fullersburg for **Benjamin Fuller** (1812-1868). Fuller platted the town that later became Hinsdale. He operated an inn on Ogden Ave., then the road to Chicago. Abraham Lincoln was reportedly a guest of the inn. Hinsdale was incorporated in 1873.

ROBERT CROWN CENTER FOR HEALTH EDUCATION, 21 Salt Creek Ln., was originally called the Hinsdale Health Museum. Its exhibits and classrooms are used for teaching general health, family living, human ecology, drug abuse, nutrition, and professional health education. It is open to the public from 2:30 to 4 p.m. weekdays, mid-September through mid-June. It is closed on holidays. An admission is charged.

DOWNERS GROVE

DOWNERS GROVE (pop. 42,691) was settled in 1832 and incorporated in 1873. It was named in honor of **Pierce Downer** (1782-1863), a prominent farmer of that era. Woodridge (pop. 21,763) lies just southwest of Downers Grove.

Several famous persons claimed Downers Grove as their hometown. Among these: **James Henry Breasted**, the internationally esteemed archaelogist, Orientalist, and Egyptologist; **Sherrill Milnes**, the highly acclaimed Verdi baritone with the Metropolitan Opera; **John A. "Shorty" Powers**, USAF officer and voice of NASA at mission control in Houston during the Mercury space flights; **Lottie Holman O'Neill**, the first woman to serve in the Illinois legislature and served there for 38 years; **Lane K. Newberry**, noted artist; and the brother-sister team of **Sterling North and Jessica North McDonald**, well-known poets and novelists.

The DOWNERS GROVE HISTORICAL MUSEUM, 831 Maple Ave., features exhibits and memorabilia relating to local history. It is open 1 to 4 p.m. Wednesday and 2 to 4 p.m. Sunday.

LISLE

LISLE (pop. 18,600), south of I-88, was settled in 1832 but was

Downers Grove is the hometown of Metropolitan opera star, Sherrill Milnes. Here Milnes appears as Count di Luna in Verdi's "Il Trovatore."

not incorporated until 1956. Until 1956 the community was called Lisle Station.

The LISLE DEPOT MUSEUM, 919 Burlington Ave., includes the 1874 C.B. & Q. Station ticket office, waiting room, History of Lisle Room and the Stationmasters' living quarters (parlor, kitchen and bedrooms). Adjacent to the museum is the 1850s Netzley/Yender Home. The noted Beaubien Tavern, c. 1840, is scheduled to be moved to this historic sites area in 1989. Owned by **Marc and Jean Baptist Beaubien**, the tavern was frequented by pioneers and Indians through Lisle. The museum is open 1 to 4 p.m. Sunday and Wednesday, April through November. Admission is free.

Located here on the campus of Illinois Benedictine College (formerly St. Procopious College, c. 1900), 5700 College Rd., is the JURICA NATURAL HISTORY MUSEUM. Named for the **Rev. Hilary S. Jurica**, the museum features an impressive collection of skeletons, including a 38-foot Rorqual whale. There are numerous mounted animals as well. It is open 12 noon to 4 p.m. Wednesday and Sunday. Admission is free.

The 1,500-acre MORTON ARBORETEUM, IL 53, was established by **Joy Morton** in 1922. This conservatory of woody plants is an outdoor museum of meadows, woodlands, prairies and formal gardens, a visitors center and "Gingko Tea Room." Morton, founder of the Morton Salt Co., gained his lifelong interest in natural history and ecology of the native landscapes from his father, **J. Sterling Morton** of Nebraska City, NE, who originated Arbor Day. The grounds are open 9 a.m. to 7 p.m. daily from May through October, and from 9 a.m. to 5 p.m. daily from November through April. The Visitors Center is open daily from 9 a.m. to 5 p.m. An admission is charged.

Joseph Naper (1798-1862) is credited with having established DuPage County while serving in the state legislature in 1839. The city of Naperville, which he helped to plat, is named in his honor and he became the first village president in 1857. Naper served as a captain in the Black Hawk War and served in the Mexican War of 1846.

NAPERVILLE

NAPERVILLE (pop. 80,000) was settled in 1831-32 and incorporated in 1857. **Fort Payne** was constructed by a detachment from Joliet under the command of **Capt. Morgan Payne** during the summer of 1832. The original fort, now part of the historical Naper Settlement, was established on the present-day site of

A scene at historic Naper Settlement in Naperville.

North Central College.

NAPER SETTLEMENT, 201 W. Porter Ave., is located on a 12 acre site near the downtown. It depicts life in this part of Illinois from the 1830s to the 1900s. Most of the 24 historical buildings have been moved from other locations in the city. The first building moved to the village museum site was the Century Memorial Chapel, dating back to 1864. Costumed guides lead tours through the village museum.

Naper Settlement is open 1:30 to 4:30 p.m. Wednesday, Saturday, and Sunday, May through October. An admission is charged.

WARRENVILLE

North of Naperville, off I-88, is WARRENVILLE (pop. 7,519). The second oldest community in the county, Warrenville is named for its founder, **Col. Julius M. Warren** (1810-93). The colonel built his home and a hotel in Warrenville. He served two terms in the state legislature.

WARRENVILLE HISTORICAL SOCIETY, 3S530 2nd St., operates a local history museum in the Albright Studio building that dates back to 1858. The building originally served as a church and school. In 1924, it housed the **Albright Gallery of Painting and Sculpture**. It is open 1 to 4 p.m. Wednesday and Sunday. It is closed during January and February. Admission is free.

West of Warrenville is **Fermi National Accelerator Laboratory**, a physics research laboratory, named in honor of **Enrico Fermi**, the Italian-American physicist who produced the first nuclear chain reaction. The world's largest atom smasher, called a synchrotron, is operated here and scientists from around the world come here to do research on atomic particles. The laboratory is physically located in DuPage County.

Also just west of Warrenville, on Eola Rd., about a quarter of a mile south of Butterfield Rd., is a historical marker on the site of the **Church of the Big and Little Woods**. Six families in the area convened at the cabin of **Thompson and Cynthia Paxton**, August 8, 1835, and organized a Presbyterian Church. This church served a wide area, St. Charles to the north and Aurora to the south. The congregation met in homes and the schoolhouse east of Batavia until 1840 when they moved to Batavia. In 1842 and 1849, the congregation helped form new churches in Aurora and Geneva.

The route along IL 19 includes the communities of Bensenville,

The Warrenville Historical Society museum is housed in the old Albright Studio Building which dates back to 1858.

Heidemann's mill, built in 1867, was one of Addison's first businesses. The windmill was 50 feet tall with a wingspread of 72 feet. It burned in 1958.

Wood Dale, Itasca, Addison, and Roselle.

BENSENVILLE

BENSENVILLE (pop. 16,106) was incorporated in 1894.

The Bensenville Historical Society has a collection in the Bensenville Public Library.

WOOD DALE

WOOD DALE (pop. 11,251) was founded in 1873 and incorporated in 1928. The Wood Dale Historical Society operates a local history museum at 7N040 Wood Dale Rd. It is open 2 to 4 p.m. Sunday.

ITASCA

ITASCA (pop. 7,129) was settled in 1843 and incorporated in 1890.

The ITASCA HISTORICAL MUSEUM is located in the original Milwaukee Road depot, built in 1873.

ADDISON

South of Itasca is ADDISON (pop. 29,826), incorporated in 1884.

The HISTORICAL MUSEUM OF ADDISON is located at 131 W. Lake St. and concentrates on local history. It is open 10 a.m. to 2 p.m. Saturday.

Roselle A. Hough (1820-92), an outstanding Chicago businessman, lived most of the time in Chicago but listed his official residence as "Bloomingdale Township." With his brother, Oramel, he built a packing house on the Chicago River. The brothers introduced the concept of using the by-products of the slaughtering business and began marketing oils and tallows and later soaps and candles. In 1865, he headed the firm that built the Union Stock Yards with the officials of 19 packing houses and a number of railroads on the board of directors. The large hotel serving the new stockyards was called the Hough House. When the hotel burned in 1912, it was replaced by the famed Stockyards Inn. In 1868 Hough built a factory in Roselle, named for the entrepreneur, to process flax into linen and rope. He built a hotel, The Beehive, where he lived for a period with workers from the factory. In 1863, Hough was elected the first president of the Chicago Chamber of Commerce. When President Lincoln's body was brought to Chicago enroute to Springfield, Hough served as grand marshal of the funeral parade.

ROSELLE

ROSELLE (pop. 17,683), named in honor of Roselle Hough, was incorporated in 1922. It was originally a section of Blooming-

Dunham Castle just west of Wayne.

dale. It was platted and recorded as the Town of Roselle in 1874.

BLOOMINGDALE

BLOOMINGDALE (pop. 12,659) was founded in 1924.

BLOOMINGDALE PARK DISTRICT MUSEUM, 108 S. Bloomingdale Rd., is housed in the oldest existing building in Bloomingdale. The museum features a gallery with changing exhibits chosen to appeal to a variety of artistic interests. It is open 10 a.m. to 2 p.m. Wednesday, 1 to 5 p.m. Thursday, 2 to 7 p.m. Friday, and 10 a.m. to 3 p.m. Saturday.

WAYNE

WAYNE (pop. 940), on Army Trail Rd. in the extreme western section of DuPage County, is one of the oldest communities in the county. In 1978, a historical district was formed which includes the Little Home Church, built in 1871, and 51 homes and buildings located on either side of Main and Glos Sts., between the C&NW railroad tracks and Powis Rd. The district has been placed in the National Register of Historic Places.

While **Dunham Castle**, corner of IL 25 and Army Trail Rd., is in Kane County, it is considered a part of Wayne. The 12,000 square-foot castle, listed on the National Register of Historical Places, is a replica of a Norman castle built in France between 1878 and 1882. It was built in 1884 under the direction of **Mark Dunham** and his wife and was initially known as the "Oaklawn Residence." It was the residence of Solomon Dunham's family after they had come from New York State in 1835. It is a private residence and not open to the public.

Chapter 8
Touring Lake County

Includes the following communities:
Deerfield
Highland Park
Highwood
Libertyville
Mundelein
North Chicago
Vernon Hills
Volo
Wauconda
Waukegan
Zion

The Museum Listings and Historical Sites
Andrew Cook Museum
Deerfield Historical Museum
Fort Sheridan
Francis Stupey Log Cabin
Great Lakes Naval Training Center
Haines House Museum
Jean Butz James Museum
Lake County Museum
Libertyville-Mundelein Historical Society
Shiloh House
Volo Antique Auto Museum and Village
Walt Durbahn Tool Museum

Chapter 8
Touring Lake County

Lake County was originally included in McHenry County, formed in 1836. Lake County was established as a separate county three years later with Burlington (now Libertyville) chosen as the county seat.

WAUKEGAN

Little Fort, renamed Waukegan in 1849, emerged in 1836 from **Little Fort Trading Post** established c. 1695. Marquette landed near present day Waukegan in 1674. The Town of Little Fort was incorporated February 19, 1841, and was selected as the new county seat, April 5, 1841. Waukegan is an Indian word meaning "fort" or "trading post."

The first newspaper to appear in what was to become Waukegan was the *Little Fort Porcupine and Democratic Banner* in 1845.

WAUKEGAN (pop. 67,653) was founded in 1841 and today is the county seat of Lake County. The courthouse was destroyed by fire in 1875 and rebuilt in 1878. **Abraham Lincoln** appeared at the **Dickinson Hotel** here in 1860 as he campaigned for the presidency.

A famous name connected with Waukegan was **Benjamin Kubelsky**, known throughout the world as **Jack Benny** (1894-1974), the radio and TV comedian. The theme of his shows was the comedy adventures of a vain, stingy, deluded man. Benny grew up in Waukegan.

Ray Bradbury, the noted science fiction writer, was born in Waukegan in 1920. Among his most noted short stories are "The Martian Chronicles" (1951), "The Illustrated Man" (1951), "A Medicine for Melancholy" (1959), and "I Sing the Body Electric" (1969). He also authored the novels, "Fahrenheit 451" (1953) and "Something Wicked This Way Comes" (1962). Bradbury has written screenplays for several motion pictures, including "Moby Dick" in 1956.

A Waukegan resident, Musician Orion P. Howe, Co. C, 55th Illinois Infantry, received the Congressional Medal of Honor for heroism at Vicksburg, Mississippi, May 19, 1863.

WAUKEGAN HISTORICAL SOCIETY is housed in the Bowen Park Haines Farmhouse, 1917 N. Sheridan Rd. Once

Photo courtesy Waukegan News-Sun

The comedian, Jack Benny, was a native of Waukegan. He often referred to his hometown during his performances.

The John C. Haines farmhouse serves as the museum operated by the Waukegan Historical Society.

Ray Bradbury, the noted science fiction author and screen writer, was born in Waukegan in 1920.

owned by the retired Chicago mayor John C. Haines, and Waukegan mayor Fred Buck, the country house was acquired by the Waukegan Park District in 1973 and leased to the historical society. The Society operates the HAINES HOUSE MUSEUM which contains artifacts and memorabilia of Waukegan pioneers. Also displayed are Indian and Civil War artifacts. It is open 10 a.m. to 3 p.m. Wednesday, Friday and Saturday. Admission is free.

ZION

North of Waukegan is ZION (pop. 17,865), founded in 1901 by **John Alexander Dowie** of the Christian Catholic Church. The Christian Catholic Church, whose members were also known as Zionites, was founded by Dowie in 1896 in Chicago. Zion was incorporated in 1902 and operated under a theocratic government until 1935. **Wilber Glenn Voliva** succeeded Dowie when he was deposed in 1906. The founder died March 9, 1907. Rev. Voliva died in 1942. Shortly after the founding of the new church, Dowie began planning for a city that was to be the headquarters for the church. During this planning period he established his headquarters in an eight story structure located on Michigan Ave. and 12th St. which also became the focal point for the "Coming City," to be called Zion. This building in Chicago was known as Zion during this period. Today, the Christian Catholic Church is

Headquarters for the Naval Training Center, Great Lakes.

located in a building, dedicated in 1961, on the Temple Site in the center of town.

ZION HISTORICAL SOCIETY, 1300 Shiloh Blvd., is housed in the 1902 Shiloh House, residence of the founder of the City of Zion. The 25-room mansion, built in the Swiss chalet style, cost $75,000. It features original furnishings and antiques. It is open 2 to 5 p.m. weekends from May through August. An admission is charged.

NORTH CHICAGO

South of Waukegan is NORTH CHICAGO (pop. 38,774), incorporated in 1909. A sit-down strike at a steel plant here in 1937 led to legal proceedings. In 1939, the U.S. Supreme Court received the case and ruled that sit-down strikes were illegal.

Great Lakes Naval Training Center, situated on 1,600 acres along the Lake Michigan shore line, was established on Sheridan Rd. just east of North Chicago, February 14, 1911. This area north of Chicago was selected from among 37 midwestern sites by a board appointed by President Theodore Roosevelt in 1904. When funds appropriated for the purchase of the original 172 acres were inadequate, the Merchants Club of Chicago raised the full amount and presented the land to the government. The first trainee was **Seaman Recruit Joseph W. Gregg. Lt. Cmdr. John Philip Sousa** directed the station bands at one time. The station's football team was national champion in 1918, defeating a Marine team in the Rose Bowl. In 1942, **Doreston Carman, Jr.** was the first black reporting for training in a general rating. In 1944, 12 ensigns and a warrant officer were commissioned after training here as the first black officers in the Navy.

During World War I, Great Lakes expanded from fewer than 50 buildings to 775 on 1,200 acres of land to provide training for more than 125,000 Navy recruits. The base was closed July 1, 1933 but reopened two years later. For a time, NTC offered flight training as well as enlisted training. The Great Lakes landing fields became inadequate and aviation training was relocated a few miles south to Glenview.

During World War II, more than a million seamen were trained here. Training reached a higher peak during the Korean Conflict when, during a seven-day period in October, 1951, more recruits were trained than during any similar period during World War II. The Vietnam era levied new demands. In 1964, 61,000 recruits graduated and in 1969, recruit numbers peaked at over 86,000.

The five component activities at the Center include the Re-

An early-day missile on display on the grounds adjacent to the Fort Sheridan Museum.

Patton Residence

2nd Lt. George S. Patton, Jr., who became famous as a general during World War II, was assigned to 15th U.S. Cavalry at Fort Sheridan upon his graduation from West Point. The post's company-grade Officer's Family Quarters occupied by the young lieutenant has been plaqued in his memory.

Patton and his wife occupied these quarters from 1909 to 1911. His daughter was born in these quarters.

This Germantown Rockaway Carriage, believed to have been used by Gen. Philip H. Sheridan on his visit to Fort Sheridan, May 10, 1888, is displayed in the Fort Sheridan Museum.

These jail cells still occupy a corridor in the Fort Sheridan Museum, once the guardhouse at the Army post.

The historic Fort Sheridan Tower was built in 1891.

cruit Training Command, Service School Command, Naval Training Station, Personnel Support Activity, and Construction Battalion Unit 401.

NTC Great Lakes provides instruction to 40 percent of all Navy recruits; offering 175 accredited courses in 11 technical schools.

Graduation ceremonies for recruits are held at 1 p.m. every Friday.

Continuing southward along the Lake Michigan shoreline is LAKE BLUFF (pop. 4,434); LAKE FOREST (pop. 15,245), settled in 1835 and incorporated in 1861; HIGHWOOD (pop. 5,455), founded in 1887; and HIGHLAND PARK (pop. 30,599).

HIGHWOOD

Fort Sheridan, just off Sheridan Rd. in Highwood, was established November 8, 1887, and officially named February 27, 1888. The first troops, units of the 6th Infantry from Fort Douglas, Utah, arrived on the 1887 date and camped in tents on uncleared land. Fort Sheridan is an important turn-of-the-century military post planned and constructed during a period of transition in national policy which signaled the closing of temporary frontier posts and the establishment of permanent garrisons of troops at strategic points throughout the United States.

The fort was named in honor of **Gen. Philip Sheridan**, who commanded troops sent to Chicago to maintain order in 1871 and again in 1877. Troops were called in during the Great Fire of 1871 and during the railroad strikes of 1877.

During the Spanish-American War, troops were sent, via Florida, to fight in Cuba. During the Philippine Insurrection, troops went to Manila to join our Army there. In 1916, Fort Sheridan soldiers joined **Gen. John "Black Jack" Pershing** in the expedition against Mexico. In 1917, the post became an officers' training camp, and later, the site of Lovell General Hospital No. 28.

In 1941, the fort was an anti-aircraft training facility and an induction-reception center. In 1945, it became a regional separation center at the end of the war. During the Korean War and Vietnam conflict, the Regular Army units here were sent to main battle areas, while the post continued as administrative and logistical support headquarters to Army activities in the midwest.

In April, 1984, the Department of Interior designated about 40 percent of Fort Sheridan acreage as a National Historic Landmark, primarily for the distinctive design of buildings dating

The Highland Park Historical Society operates three museums including the Jean Butz James Museum shown here.

back to 1890. Information is available at the museum.

(In 1989, an announcement was made in Washington that this historic fort was one of several military installations across the country to be closed within the next two years.)

FORT SHERIDAN MUSEUM, Bldg. 33 at Fort Sheridan, is housed in a one-story building originally used as a post stockade, dating back to 1890. It is one of 94 buildings in a National Historic Landmark District. It traces the history of the Army and Fort Sheridan through a collection of firearms and uniforms as well as other equipment used by soldiers. **George S. Patton** served on guard duty here at the outset of his career, 1909-11. It is open 10 a.m. to 4 p.m. daily. It is closed New Year's Day, Presidents' Day, Labor Day, Columbus Day, Thanksgiving, and Christmas. Admission is free.

HIGHLAND PARK

Highland Park was settled in 1834 and incorporated in 1869.

The HIGHLAND PARK HISTORICAL SOCIETY, 326 Central Ave., Highland Park, operates three museums. The JEAN BUTZ JAMES MUSEUM serves as the Society's headquarters. The 10-room brick Victorian house dates back to 1871. Featured are exhibits and memorabilia depicting frontier life in the area and community history. The WALT DURBAHN TOOL MUSEUM is also on the grounds. The third museum is the FRANCIS STUPEY LOG CABIN, dating back to 1847. It is located in Laurel Park. These museums are open 10 a.m. to 5 p.m. Tuesday through Friday and from 2 to 4 p.m. weekends and holidays. Admission is free.

DEERFIELD

Just west of Highland Park is DEERFIELD (pop. 17,432), incorporated in 1903.

DEERFIELD HISTORICAL MUSEUM, 450 Kipling Pl., highlights local history. It is open 2 to 4 p.m. Sunday, May through October.

LIBERTYVILLE (pop. 16,520), MUNDELEIN (pop. 17,053), and VERNON HILLS (pop. 9,827), can be reached by driving north on I-294 and I-94 and taking IL 176 west.

LIBERTYVILLE-MUNDELEIN-VERNON HILLS

In its history Libertyville was called Independence Grove and then renamed Burlington when it became the new county's first county seat.

Mundelein was formed as a settlement called Mechanics Grove in 1835. It was named Holcomb in 1850, then Rockefeller in 1886.

The Libertyville-Mundelein Historical Society is housed in the 1876 residence of Ansel B. Cook in Libertyville.

Oldest Church in the County

The oldest church in Lake County is located just west of Mundelein, in nearby Ivanhoe, on Route 176. This early Congregational Church, established in February 1838, is listed on the Illinois Register of Historic Places.

In 1909 it was renamed Area for the world's largest correspondence school which settled on 600 acres of woods surrounding a lake. When the school went into bankruptcy, the Catholic Archdiocese purchased the land and built St. Mary of the Lake Seminary under the direction of **George Cardinal Mundelein**. In 1926, the village was renamed Mundelein in his honor.

Vernon Hills was first settled in 1835. **Albert B. Steele** was the first white child born in Lake County, June 20, 1835, in Vernon Hills.

The historical attractions in this area:

LIBERTYVILLE-MUNDELEIN HISTORICAL SOCIETY, 413 N. Milwaukee Ave., Libertyville, is housed in the 1876 Victorian residence of **Ansel B. Cook**. It features items dating back to the Civil War, historical books and photos and other memorabilia. It is open 2 to 4 p.m. Sundays during the summer. Admission is free.

WAUCONDA

West of Mundelein on Bangs Lake, via IL 176, is WAUCONDA (pop. 5,688). Settled by the **Justice Bang** family in 1836, Wauconda was incorporated in 1877. According to legend, Wauconda, an Indian word meaning "spirit waters," was named for a young Indian chief who is buried somewhere on the southern shore of Bangs Lake.

The historical attractions here:

LAKE COUNTY MUSEUM, on IL 176 (Liberty St., east of town in the Lake County Forest Preserve), traces the cultural and geographic changes in Lake County from the earliest known inhabitants to the 20th century. Of special interest is the Curt Teich 1.5 million postcard collection, dating from 1898-1975. It was given to the museum in 1982 by Regensteiner Publishing Enterprises, Inc. of Chicago. The Forest Preserve acquired the property, a 1,250 acre dairy and cattle breeding farm from 1925, in 1969. The museum is housed in what was the cattle barn. It is open 1 to 4:30 p.m. daily. It is closed New Year's Day, Thanksgiving, and Christmas. An admission is charged.

ANDREW COOK MUSEUM, 711 N. Main St., is housed in the 1840 brick residence of **Andrew C. Cook**, a prominent farmer, and is operated by the Wauconda Township Historical Society. It features farm equipment, furniture, cow bells, Civil War cavalry equipment and other items. It is open 2 to 4 p.m. Sundays, May through October. An admission is charged.

Lake County Museum is located in this building in the Lake County Forest Preserve just east of Wauconda.

The Andrew Cook Museum is housed in this 1840 brick residence on North Main Street in Wauconda.

VOLO

North of Wauconda about five miles, via US 12, is unincorporated Volo and the VOLO ANTIQUE AUTO MUSEUM AND VILLAGE. Located at 27640 W. Hwy 120, the museum features 70 antique automobiles, motorcycles and a steam tractor. Also included is a blacksmith shop, print shop, jail, and gasoline filling station. It is open 10 a.m. to 5 p.m. daily. It is closed New Year's Day, Easter, Thanksgiving and Christmas. An admission is charged.

Chapter 9
Touring McHenry County

Includes the following communities:
Crystal Lake
Harvard
Hebron
Marengo
McHenry
Richmond
Union
Woodstock

The Museum Listings and Historic Sites
Illinois Railway Museum
Lakeland (Home of Charles S. Dole)
McHenry County Historical Society Museum
The Palmer House
Seven Acres Antique Village and Museum
Woodstock Opera House

Chapter 9
Touring McHenry County

McHenry County was named in honor of **Col. William McHenry**, a veteran of the Blackhawk War. Initially the county seat was located in the village of McHenry. It was moved to its present location in 1844.

One of the county's first communities was a settlement west of McHenry known as Ostend. All that remains today is the Ostend Cemetery, once called the Thompson Burying Grounds. It was established in 1842 upon the death of Lucinda Thompson, who died in December, that year. The last burial in the cemetery was that of Charles Jecks in 1955. Ostend once had a post office, a school, creamery and Thompson Inn.

Henry Weston is believed to have been the first white settler to the area, arriving in 1833.

WOODSTOCK

WOODSTOCK (pop. 11,725) is the county seat of McHenry County. It was laid out in 1844 and incorporated in 1852. It can be reached by US 14 or IL 176, 120 and 47 (off I-90), about an hours travel time from Chicago. Woodstock was originally called Centerville and was the county's second county seat. It was renamed in 1844 for Woodstock, Vermont, the native home of several of the early settlers.

Woodstock's Opera House, on the Square, has a rich history. **Orson Welles** appeared in his first Shakespearian role here. Other famous alumni who began their careers here are **Paul Newman, Shelley Berman, Tom Bosley, Geraldine Page, Betsy Palmer,** and **Lois Nettleton**. The opera house has been restored to its 1890s splendor and stages a variety of shows every year. It is listed on the National Register of Historic Places.

Across the square is the Old Courthouse and Jail, dating back to 1857. Labor leader Eugene Debs, involved in the Pullman strike in 1894, was once held in the jail here. It is listed on the National Register of Historic Places. In the 1970s the complex was converted into a restaurant, ice cream parlor and a series of specialty shops.

For years, **Chester Gould**, creator of the comic strip character, Dick Tracy, developed episode after episode in the career of his square-jawed, trench-coated detective out of his studio in Wood-

Chester Gould, creator of the Dick Tracy cartoon strip, worked out of a studio in Woodstock for many years.

stock. Among a few of the villians Tracy faced were Stooge Viller, Influence, Blowtop, The Mole, Pruneface, 88 Keyes, Brow, Mumbles, Flattop, Haf and Haf, Angeltop, and Torcher. The idea for the comic strip came to Gould because of the hoodlum element that was so prominent in Chicago between 1921 to 1931. He attended the Art Institute of Chicago for one term and began drawing his first regular cartoon strip, "Fillum Fables," in 1923 for Hearst newspapers. Gould drew his last Dick Tracy strip, December 24, 1977, when he turned it over to the *Chicago Tribune-New York News Syndicate* and a pair of collaborators. The

The McHenry County Historical Society Museum is located in the 1870 Union School building in Union.

Seven Acres Antique Village and Museum, near Union, includes a section called "Old West Town," where "Wild West" shows are held regularly during the summer months.

cartoon strip first appeared on Sunday, October 4, 1931, in the old *Detroit Mirror*.

The City has arranged three walking tours through Woodstock. For a map for any or all of these three tours, please contact the City Clerk's office.

HEBRON

North of Woodstock is HEBRON (pop. 786), hometown of Congressional Medal of Honor recipient WT1/c Elmer C. Bigelow, USNR. Bigelow was awarded the CMH for conspicuous gallantry while serving aboard the *U.S.S. Fletcher* during action against the Japanese off Corregidor Island, February 14, 1945.

RICHMOND

Just east of Hebron is RICHMOND (pop. 1,068) hometown of Seaman Hugh P. Mullin, USN, who was awarded the Congressional Medal of Honor for saving the life of a comrade at Hampton Roads, Virginia, November 11, 1899.

UNION

Southwest of Woodstock is UNION (pop. 662), home of the McHENRY COUNTY HISTORICAL SOCIETY MUSEUM. Union can be reached by driving three miles south on IL 47 and then west on IL 176. The museum is housed in the 1870 Union School and offers a comprehensive collection of artifacts detailing the history and growth of the county. The log cabin in front of the museum was built in 1847. The museum is open 1:30 to 4:30 p.m. Wednesday and Sunday, during the months of May, September and October. It is open during the same hours on Wednesday and weekends through June, July and August. There is an admission charge.

The ILLINOIS RAILWAY MUSEUM is located just outside Union on Olson Rd. The museum features over 200 pieces of various railway equipment, including steam and diesel locomotives, trolleys, streetcars, interurban cars and other rolling railway stock. The collection includes a horse car built in 1859, weighing four tons and powered by one horse, to the 400 steam engine that produced 6,000 horsepower. Trolley and train rides are offered. It is open 10 a.m. to 4 p.m. weekdays and 10:30 a.m. to 5:30 p.m. weekends, Memorial Day through Labor Day; 10:30 a.m. to 5:30 p.m. weekends, May and September; and 10:30 a.m. to 5 p.m. Sunday, in April and October. It is closed November through April. There is an admission charge.

SEVEN ACRES ANTIQUE VILLAGE AND MUSEUM is another museum in the Union area. It is located at 8512 S. Union

A member of the cast of the "Wild West" show at Seven Acres Antique Village and Museum near Union.

Exhibits at the Illinois Railway Museum in Union.

182

Rd. The museum boasts one of the country's largest collections of Thomas Edison phonographs as well as cylinder and disc music machines. The museum also features a World War II military exhibit including rare uniforms, weapons, Japanese and German medals, to a special collection that once belonged to man who rode with Lawrence of Arabia. Numerous other exhibits are on display in the museum. A Western village features live entertainment and stores. It is open 9 a.m. to 6 p.m. daily, May through September and 10 a.m. to 5 p.m. weekends only in April and October. Closed November through March. There is an admission charge.

MARENGO

West of Union, via IL 176, is MARENGO (pop. 4,361). It is on US 20. Marengo was home to **Egbert Anson Van Alstyne** (1882-1951), who wrote the music for such hits as "Pretty Baby," "Drifting and Dreaming," "That Old Girl of Mine," and "In the Shade of the Old Apple Tree."

CRYSTAL LAKE

South of Woodstock is CRYSTAL LAKE (pop. 18,950), settled in 1836 and incorporated as a village in 1874. That same year, the settlement north of Crystal Lake Ave. was incorporated as Nunda, later called North Crystal Lake, and the towns merged in 1914. It is the largest city in McHenry county.

Screen and TV actor **Bruce Boxleitner** was born in 1950 and lived in Crystal Lake until he was 10 years old.

Crystal Lake has two historic buildings, including the Palmer House, on Terra Cotta Rd., and Lakeland or the Dole Mansion at 401 Country Club Rd.

Lakeland was the name **Charles S. Dole**, a wealthy Chicago grain merchant, bestowed on his 450-acre estate on the lake in the 1860s. In 1866, Dole laid out a half mile race track at Lakeland and purchased some of the finest horses money could buy. Later, he became interested in dairy cattle. Dole maintained his estate for 34 years and entertained lavishly. One of the most elaborate weddings in the West was held here in 1883. It was the scene of the wedding of Dole's daughter, Mary Frances, to Albert C. Stowell of Nebraska. A special train brought 300 wedding guests from Chicago to Lakeland on Dole's private spur line to the lake. The mansion is being restored.

The Col. Palmer residence was built in 1858 for **Col. Gustavius and Henriette Palmer**. Palmer had served as a colonel in the 205th New York Infantry, which took part in the little-

Bruce Boxleitner, popular screen and TV star, was born in Crystal Lake. He starred in the TV series, "Scarecrow and Mrs. King," and leading roles in other film productions.

known Patriot's War of 1837-38. It is believed he received bounty lands in Illinois for his military services. Eighty acres of land in McHenry County were issued to Palmer in an 1845 land patent. The Palmers died within three days of each other in December, 1884. The home is located on IL 176 at Terra Cotta Rd. It is listed on the National Register of Historic Places.

McHENRY

McHENRY (pop. 14,000) is north of Crystal Lake via IL 31 and east of Woodstock via IL 120. It was the first seat of government when Lake County was part of McHenry County. The first settlers arrived in 1836. McHenry is called the "Gateway to the Chain O'Lakes." Estates, which were once the waterfront summer homes of the Chicagoland wealthy, are now gracious year-round homes. McHenry offers a historic walking/driving tour involving twenty nine structures (please note, the residences listed in the brochure, available through the chamber of commerce, are private and visitors are asked to respect the privacy of the occupants). The Count's Home, 3803 W. Waukegan Rd., dates back to the 1860s and is listed on the National Register of Historic Places. The oldest residence is the Owens Home, 1113 N. 4th St., dating back to 1838.

North of McHenry, via IL 31, is Richmond. Called the Antique Hub of Northern Illinois, the antique shops are located in turn-of-the-century buildings in the downtown area.

HARVARD

HARVARD (pop. 5,126) is 10 miles northwest of Woodstock, via US 14. It was laid out in 1856.

The GREATER HARVARD AREA HISTORICAL SOCIETY operates the Harvard History Museum at 308 N. Hart Blvd. The museum houses several collections that tell the story of the Harvard area. The historical society and museum are located in the former Congregational Church, built in 1866. It is open 1:30 to 4 p.m. Sundays from May through September. Admission is free.

The historic Dole Mansion in Crystal Lake was the scene of "one of the most brilliant weddings in the West." Charles S. Dole called his estate Lakeland.

Col. Gustavius and Henriette Palmer built this beautiful home in 1858 on the corner of Terra Cotta Rd. and IL 176 in Crystal Lake.

Chapter 10
Touring Kane County

Includes the following communities:
Aurora
Batavia
Campton Township
The Dundees
Elgin
Geneva
St. Charles
South Elgin
Virgil

The Museum Listings and Historic Sites

Aurora Fire Museum
Aurora Historical Museum
Aurora Police Department Museum
Batavia Depot Museum
Bellevue Place
Blackberry Historical Farm/Village
Dundee Township Historical Museum
Dunham-Hunt Museum
Durant-Peterson House/Pioneer Sholes School
Elgin Area Historical Museum
Elgin National Road Race Memorial
Elgin Public Museum
Fabyan Villa Museum
Fermi National Accelerator Laboratory
Fox River Trolley Museum
GAR Memorial and Veteran's Military Museum
Garfield Farm Museum
Geneva Historical Society Museum
Haeger Museum
Langum Park
Near Eastside Historic District (Aurora)
Near Northwest Historic District (Aurora)
Paramount Arts Center
Pinkerton House
Quereau House
St. Charles Historical Society Museum
Stolp Island Historic District (Aurora)
Sri Vendateswara Swami Temple of Greater Chicago
Westside Historic District (Aurora)

Chapter 10
Touring Kane County

The two major highways through Kane county are I-90 and I-88. The two principal cities are Aurora (pop. 81,293), just off I-88 and Elgin (pop. 69,618), just off I-90, both about 40 miles west of Chicago. The other major towns are Batavia, Geneva, St. Charles, South Elgin, East Dundee, West Dundee, and Carpentersville. Aurora, Elgin, Batavia, Geneva, St. Charles, South Elgin, and East and West Dundee are set along the Fox River and are connected by IL 31.

AURORA

AURORA was settled in 1834 and incorporated in 1837. It was one of the first cities to use electricity for street lights. The **Illinois Mathematics and Science Academy**, 1500 Sullivan Rd., geared for students with exceptional aptitude in math and science, opened in 1986. It is one of only three of its kind in the U.S. Public tours are not available.

The eastern part of the city lies on the east bank of the Fox River and is located in DuPage county.

Three Congressional Medal of Honor recipients have come from Aurora. 2nd Lt. Walter E. Truemper, 8th Air Force, received the medal for action over Europe, February 20, 1944; Pfc James H. Monroe, 1st Cavalry Division, for gallantry at Bong Son, Hoai Nhon Province, Vietnam, February 16, 1967; and L/Cpl. Lester W. Weber, USMC, 1st Marine Division, for heroism at Quang Nam Province, Vietnam, February 23, 1969.

Historical attractions in the Aurora area:

AURORA HISTORICAL MUSEUM, 305 Cedar St., Aurora, is housed in an 1857 mansion with an adjoining carriage house. It is listed on the National Register of Historic Places. It features local and area history and among its many exhibits are 10,000-year old mastodon skeletal remains. On display is William Blanford's nine-foot astronomical clock, dating back to 1905, which keeps time, the date, and the times in various cities of the world. The clock, called a scientific wonder, was set to run accurately for thousands of years. The offerings are typical of local museums. It is open 1 to 5 p.m., Wednesdays and weekends, February through December 24, and other times by appointment. The carriage house is open 1 to 5 p.m. weekends, May through October. An ad-

This 1857 mansion houses the Aurora Historical Museum.

The GAR Memorial and Veteran's Military Museum is located at 23 E. Downer Pl. in Aurora.

mission is charged.

GRAND ARMY OF THE REPUBLIC MEMORIAL AND VETERAN'S MILITARY MUSEUM, 23 E. Downer Pl., Aurora, includes military displays from the Civil War, Spanish American War, World War I, World War II, Korean Conflict, and Vietnam War. The museum is housed in an 1877 sandstone building. It is listed on the National Register of Historic Places. It is open 12 noon to 4 p.m., Monday, Wednesday, and Friday. Admission is free.

AURORA FIRE MUSEUM, 800 Michaels St., No. 4 Fire Station, features a collection of uniforms, equipment, and photos. It is open 9 a.m. to 5 p.m. daily with advance reservations, (call 898-3655). Admission is free.

AURORA POLICE DEPARTMENT MUSEUM, 350 N. River St., housed in the Aurora Police Department, traces the history of police work in Aurora through artifacts, photos, and memorabilia. Tours are available with advance reservations, (call 859-1700). Admission is free.

The historic machine shops of a pre-Civil War railroad have been renovated into a **Regional Transportation Center** at 233 N. Broadway. The adjacent roundhouse, dating from 1855-65, is the oldest, full roundhouse in the country and the only stone roundhouse remaining in the U.S. The National Park Service has deemed the complex "of pre-eminent importance in American transportation history" and has listed it on the National Register of Historic Places. These structures are all that remained of the 60-plus acre site which was the construction and repair yards for what is now the Burlington Northern Railroad. Food and beverage and other services are available on the site. The building is open 5:30 a.m. to 8:30 p.m. daily.

Memorial Bridge, crossing the Fox River via New York St., is a reinforced structure designed in an Art Deco "depression style" motif. Rather than simply using commemorative statuary, Emory Seidel designed the entire bridge as a memorial to World War I veterans. The two cast concrete pairs of kneeling statues, on either side of the bridge, represent "Memory" and the large bronze statue in the center of the span represents "Victory." The bridge, dedicated on Armistice Day in 1931, also features specially designed balusters and ornamental lighting standards.

The Paramount Arts Center, 23 E. Galena Blvd., was constructed in 1931 by Rapp and Rapp in keeping with the opulent movie palaces of the era. The theatre was restored in 1978 as a performing arts center offering a full season of professional entertainment. Tours are available with advance reservations, (call 896-7676). Admission is charged.

The locally designated Near Eastside Historic District, bound by Galena, Seminary and S. 4th Sts., and S. Lincoln Ave., is a collection of over 350 homes which date from the mid-to-late 19th century. It includes excellent examples of Greek Revival, Italianate, and Queen Anne style residential architecture. Self guided tour brochures are available at the Convention & Tourism Council, 40 W. Downer Pl.

Westside Historic District, bound by W. Downer Pl., S. Lake St., and Garfield and S. Highland Aves., was first platted in the 1840s. The W. Downer Place neighborhood has traditionally been the choice of industrialists and community leaders. The large, elegant houses in this area date from 1856 to 1922. The most popular architectural styles from this time are represented from the many Victorian styles to the picturesque Revival styles of the 1919-20s. The district was listed on the National Register of Historic Places in 1986. Self guided tour brochures are available at the Convention & Tourism Council, 40 W. Downer Pl.

Twenty-eight homes are listed on the Near Northwest Historic District walking tour. Self guided tour brochures are available at the Convention & Tourism Council, 40 W. Downer Pl.

Among the buildings in Aurora listed on the National Register of Historic Places are Healy Chapel, 332 W. Downer Pl.; Copley Mansion, 434 W. Downer Pl.; the Aurora Hotel, 2 N. Stolp Ave.; the Keystone Building, 30 Stolp Ave.; the Graham Building, 33-35 S. Stolp Ave.; the Grand Army of the Republic (GAR) Memorial Hall, 23 E. Downer Pl.; and the Stolp Woolen Mill Store, 65 S. Stolp Ave.

Stolp Island, in the Fox River, served as the connecting link between the east and west sides of town in the early days. **Joseph Stolp** bought the island for $12 and started building his woolen mill here in 1848. The island became the "neutral" territory between the east and west sides of town so it was here Aurora's early public buildings and other private organizations were located.

The Stolp Island Historic District, listed on the National Register of Historic Places in 1986, is a significant collection of late 19th and early 20th century structures. Over 30 structures comprise this district which has been called an outdoor museum of terra cotta. Self guided tour brochures are available at the

The Batavia Depot, housing the local museum, dates back to 1854.

The Geneva Historical Museum is located in Wheeler Park on IL. Rt. 31.

Convention & Tourism Council. 40 W. Downer Pl.

The **Quereau House**, 149 S. 4th St., is significant because of one of its occupants. Dr. Quereau was a prominent Aurora educator and managed the Aurora Silver Plate Company. He was a fellow voyager of Mark Twain's during his travels through Europe and the Middle East, and may be the professor Twain describes in "Innocents Abroad."

Sri Vendateswara Swami Temple of Greater Chicago, 1145 W. Sullivan Rd., is one of only three Sri Vendateswara Hindu temples in the U.S., currently (1989) under construction by Indian artisans. When completed, the temple will house a visitors center and cultural center. It is open 9 a.m. to 1 p.m. and 5 to 9 p.m. weekdays, 9 a.m. to 9 p.m. weekends. Admission is free.

BLACKBERRY HISTORICAL FARM—VILLAGE, Barnes Rd. and Galena, Aurora, depicts turn-of-the-century rural life in the Midwest. It is a living farm-village located on 60-acres. Featured are several old stores, restored coaches and sleighs, and other buildings and exhibits depicting the period. Special events are scheduled during the year. It is open 10 a.m. to 4:30 p.m. daily, May through Labor Day, and the same hours Friday through Sundays, Labor Day through October. An admission is charged.

BATAVIA

Driving north on IL 31 is BATAVIA (pop. 15,684), settled c. 1834 and incorporated in 1856. Batavia, nicknamed the "Windmill City," was home to three major windmill manufacturers whose product was shipped world wide. **Fermi National Accelerator Laboratory** is located on the eastern edge of Batavia.

Batavia native Thomas A. Pope was awarded the Congressional Medal of Honor during World War I. Corporal Pope, Co. E, 131st Infantry, was decorated for heroism at Hamel, France, July 4, 1918.

BATAVIA DEPOT MUSEUM, 155 Houston, Batavia, is one of the oldest (1854) railroad stations on the Burlington Railroad. Among its exhibits is a Mary Todd Lincoln display. It is listed on the National Register of Historic Places. It is open 2 to 4 p.m., Monday, Wednesday, Friday, and weekends. Admission is free.

Bellevue Place, west on Union St., off IL 31, is identified with a historical marker. Originally built as a school in the 1850s, it became a rest home and sanitarium in 1867. In the summer of 1875, the unstable **Mary Todd Lincoln**, widow of President Lincoln, was a patient at Bellevue Place.

This historical marker in Langum Park, St. Charles, commemorates Camp Kane, organized in 1861 as a military training camp for Union soldiers recruited from the area.

Mary Todd Lincoln, widow of President Lincoln, was once a patient at Bellevue Place, a Batavia sanitarium.

The former Col. George and Nelle Fabyan estate, located on the Fox River in Geneva, is owned by the Kane County Forest Preserve District. The Fabyan Villa Museum, a 1907 Frank Lloyd Wright design, contains a natural history collection and Fabyan memorabilia. George Fabyan became wealthy in the cotton textile business. He had several other interests, including research in various areas.

ILLINOIS IS FROM INDIAN WORD

The early-day French settlers who came to the region named it for the Illinois, or Illini, Indians. The Indians here called themselves Illiniwek (superior men). The name Illinois came from the French pronunciation of Illiniwek.

GENEVA

Continuing north on IL 31 is GENEVA (pop. 9,881), the county seat. Geneva was settled in c. 1833 and incorporated in 1867. **Gower Champion** (1919-80), best known as a choreographer, was born in Geneva. He also was a stage, screen, vaudeville and TV actor, film and stage director.

There are some 200 landmarks in Geneva and the list is available at the chamber of commerce.

The historical attractions in the county seat:

GENEVA HISTORICAL SOCIETY MUSEUM, in Wheeler Park on IL 31, Geneva, provides exhibits and displays from early pioneer days to the turn-of-the-century. These are displayed in three exhibit rooms. A resource center is provided for limited research. It is open 2 to 4:30 p.m., Wednesdays and weekends, April through December. Donations are accepted.

FABYAN VILLA MUSEUM, 1511 S. Batavia Ave., is located in the 235-acre Fabyan Forest Preserve along the Fox River in Geneva. It is housed in the 1907 home designed by **Frank Lloyd Wright** for **Col. George Fabyan**. A wealthy cotton textile businessman, Fabyan conducted research in acoustics, cryptology, physical fitness, livestock breeding, and plant genetics in his laboratories. Riverbank Laboratories, on the west side of IL 31, are used for acoustic research and development by Illinois Institute of Technology and IIT Research Institute, under a Fabyan trust. It is listed on the National Register of Historic Places. The Fabyan Museum is open 1 to 4 p.m. weekends and holidays, May through mid October, and other times by appointment. Admission is free.

CAMPTON TOWNSHIP

Five miles west of Geneva, on IL 38 and Garfield Rd. (in Campton Township), is GARFIELD FARM MUSEUM. This 1840s farm and teamster inn is being restored and developed as an 1840s working farm. It is listed on the National Register of Historic Places. The tour includes an 1846 inn, 1842 and 1849 barns, a reconstructed 1847 poultry house and historic poultry flock and prairie restoration. It is open 1 to 4 p.m. Wednesdays and Sundays, June through September. Admission is charged.

ST. CHARLES

Just north of Geneva is ST. CHARLES (pop. 19,500), originally called Charleston. Part of the town lies east across the river in DuPage county. It was settled in 1833 and incorporated in 1838.

A statue honoring the Pottawatomi Indians was erected and dedicated in 1915. The Pottawatomi inhabited the Fox River Valley at least 100 years before white men arrived. They were generally peaceful Indians who befriended the white settlers. The 1915 statue was destroyed by vandals in 1965. A new statue, on the east side of the Fox River, a few hundred feet north of the Main Street bridge, was dedicated May 22, 1988.

Composer **Dave Bennett**, born in 1897, has been a resident of St. Charles for many years and has appeared regularly at the St. Charles Rotary Club Thursday luncheon meetings to lead the singing of "Bye Bye Blues," perhaps his most popular song. He also wrote "Rhapsody in Rhumba," "Repartee," and "Cubana."

Screen and stage actor **Charles Clary** (1873-1931) was born in St. Charles.

Pvt. Andrew E. Goldsberry, Co. E, 127th Illinois Infantry, was awarded the Congressional Medal of Honor for heroism at Vicksburg, Mississippi, May 22, 1863. He was a native of St. Charles.

Probably the community's greatest benefactors were **Dellora Angell Norris and Edward John Baker**, heirs of **John Warne "Bet-A-Million" Gates**, who turned barbed wire and oil into gold (the gold in the form of Texaco Oil stock). Gates was the founder of Texaco. His fame (and fortune) began as a salesman for **Joseph Glidden**, who invented barbed wire. Young Gates went to San Antonio, Texas, and bet skeptical cattlemen that 40 of their Texas longhorns could not fight their way out of a barbed wire enclosure he setup in the town plaza. When night fell and the enraged cattle were still unable to escape, the boom started. Gates sold hundreds of miles of Glidden wire and skyrocketed to success. He bought up wire companies around the country and organized the American Steel and Wire Company, which became part of the the US Steel combine. He later became interested and involved in the oil business.

Among the historical attractions in St. Charles:

DUNHAM-HUNT MUSEUM, 304 Cedar Ave., was built in 1840 by **Bela Hunt**, an early-day settler. It is furnished with items from Mark W. Dunham's "Dunham Castle," built in 1884, by the famous horse importer. It is listed on the National Register of Historic Places. The restored law office of S. S. Jones, built in 1843, was moved to the museum grounds in July, 1988, and is now part of the complex. The museum is open 1 to 4 p.m. Wednesday through Sunday, but closed on holidays. Admission is free except for tours when a modest admission is charged.

This statue in St. Charles honors the Pottawatomi Indians who once occupied lands in the Fox River Valley.

The Dunham-Hunt Museum is located in the 1840 St. Charles home of Bela Hunt, an early settler.

The St. Charles Historical Society Museum is located in the Municipal Building in St. Charles.

The Durant-Peterson House, built in 1843, and the pioneer Sholes School (below) are located in the LeRoy Oakes Forest Preserve, just north of St. Charles.

ST. CHARLES HISTORICAL SOCIETY MUSEUM, 2 E. Main St. (Municipal Building), includes artifacts from the Civil War period, Indian arrowheads found in the area, and a collection of over 4,000 photographs that recaptures the development of the community. It is open 12 noon to 4 p.m. Monday through Sunday, May through September, and the same hours Monday through Friday, October through April. Admission is free.

The DURANT-PETERSON HOUSE, in LeRoy Oakes Forest Preserve, Dean St. near Randall Rd., depicts rural life in the 1840s in the Midwest. Visitors are taken through the 1843 prairie house by costumed guides. It is listed on the National Register of Historic Places. It is open 1 to 4 p.m. Sundays, June 15 through October 15. Special tours are available by appointment. Admission is free.

PIONEER SHOLES SCHOOL, in LeRoy Oakes Forest Preserve, Dean St., near Randall Rd., is a restored one room school on display that also serves as a living museum for students and teachers to re-enact turn of the century classes. Collection of 19th and early 20th century school texts, early official Kane County education records, oral histories of one room schools, programs on education and preservation. It is open 1 to 4 p.m. Sundays, May through October. Classes/groups by appointment. Admission is free.

LANGUM PARK, on IL 25, in the south part of St. Charles, was the site of **Camp Kane**, a training camp for the 8th and 17th Illinois Cavalry during the Civil War. At the outbreak of the war, the population of St. Charles was 2,284 persons. Congressman **John Franklin Farnsworth**, a resident of St. Charles, was authorized to raise a cavalry regiment and quickly recruited 1,200 men for this purpose. The 8th was organized in September, 1861, by Farnsworth, commissioned a colonel and given command of the regiment that served with the Army of the Potomac. Normal strength of the regiment was 1,200 but during its tour of duty 2,412 names appeared on its rolls. Casualties in the regiment included 194 killed or died, 185 wounded, and 11 died as prisoners in Confederate POW camps. The 17th was organized in 1863 by **Col. John L. Beveridge**. The regiment was involved in the capture of 900 Confederates at the Battle of Mine Creek, the only Civil War battle fought in Kansas, on October 25, 1864. It also saw action in several skirmishes in Missouri that fall.

The 1928 Baker Hotel, 100 W. Main, is listed on the National Register of Historic Places. The hotel today serves as a senior

Noted sculptor Trygve A. Rovelstad, born in Elgin in 1903, served as an assistant under Lorado Taft. Among his many works was the design for the Elgin (Ill.) Half Dollar, minted in 1936 to commemorate the city's centennial year. His specialty has been historical figures. His home and studios (in 1989) are in Elgin.

THE ILLINOIS STATE FLOWER
The Illinois State flower is the Native Violet.

citizen residence operated by Lutheran Social Services of Illinois.

VIRGIL

West of St. Charles, via IL 64, is unincorporated VIRGIL, hometown of Congressional Medal of Honor recipient Cpl. Wesley J. Powers, Co. F, 147th Illinois Infantry, for heroism at Oostanaula, Georgia, April 3, 1865.

ELGIN

Off I-90, to the north, is ELGIN (pop. 69,618), settled in 1835 and incorporated in 1847. Elgin is home of **Elgin Academy**, a coeducational preparatory school, founded in 1839.

The Elgin Automobile Road Race Association was incorporated in 1910 and sponsored the **Elgin National Road Races**. The Chicago Motor Club, who held a disappointing race at Crown Point, Indiana, a year earlier, endorsed the Elgin association's efforts. The road race course in Elgin covered nearly eight and a half miles with no steep hills, railroad crossings or other towns to pass through. The route generally followed today's Larkin Ave., McLean Blvd, Highland Ave., and Coombs Rd. The first 305-mile Elgin National, held August 27, 1910, was won by **Ralph Mulford** who drove his Lozier an average of 62.5 miles per hour. These races were held annually in 1911, 1912, 1913, 1914, 1915, 1919 and 1920 and revived one more time in 1933. Famous racers who competed here were **Barney Oldfield**, **Tommy Milton**, **Al Livingston**, **Ray Harroun**, and **Eddie Rickenbacker**. The most consistent winner was **Ralph DePalma**, who won the race in 1912, 1913, 1914, and 1920.

The most spectacular, fatal crash occurred during the 1914 race, when **Spencer Wishart** and his mechanic, **Jack Jenter**, were killed when the driver lost control of his Mercer. Of the 28 starters in this race, only five finished. A road rally commemorating this event is now an annual event in Elgin during the month of August. Vintage cars travel paved country back roads and trophies are awarded. For further details contact the Elgin Area Convention and Visitors Bureau, 741-5660.

Among the personalities, with roots in Elgin, are **James M. Roche**, former chief executive officer and chairman of the board of General Motors, Corp., and the late **Earl "Madman" Muntz** (1914-87), hailed by *Newsweek* magazine as "the master used-car salesman of all time." Roche joined General Motors in 1927, at the age of 21, and worked his way through Cadillac division until 1960 when he became responsibile for the entire marketing activi-

Super Salesman "Mad Man" Muntz got his start in Elgin.

A native Elginite. . .James M. Roche, former GM chairman.

"Old Main," on the campus of Elgin Academy, is home of the Elgin Area Historical Museum.

This memorial tablet is located on Fire Station 4 property, 1555 Larkin Ave. in Elgin, to commemorate the first Elgin National Road Race, held August 27, 1910. Ralph Mulford, driving a Lozier automobile, drove 62.5 mph to win the 36-lap, 305-mile classic. Nine race meets were held over the eight-mile Elgin track from 1910 to 1915, in 1919 and 1920, and in 1933. In the photo (left, kneeling) is E. C. Alft, former mayor of the City of Elgin and a noted area historian.

ties for General Motors. He was elected GM president in 1965 and chairman of the board and CEO in 1967. Muntz became famous for selling cars in California using the line, "I want to give them away, but Mrs. Muntz won't let me. She's crazy." He built the first American sports car, the Muntz Jet, and sold 394 claiming to have lost $1,000 on each sale. He made and lost several fortunes.

Among the historical attractions in Elgin:

ELGIN AREA HISTORICAL MUSEUM is housed in the

1856 "Old Main" building on the Elgin Academy campus, 360 Park St. It is the first building in Elgin to be listed as a National Historic Site. Still being developed, the museum features local and area history in its presentations. It is open noon to 4 p.m., Wednesday through Saturday. An admission is charged.

ELGIN PUBLIC MUSEUM, 225 Grand Blvd. (in Lord's Park), is the area's oldest museum, established in 1904 by **Mr. and Mrs. G. P. Lord** of Elgin. During its first two decades, the museum was operated by the Elgin Area Audubon Society. Today, its collections include approximately 15,000 accession quality natural history specimens. A strong interpretive collection of Native American Indian objects has been developed. Other interpretive collections include Illinois Wildlife, Fish of Illinois, Butterflies and Insects, and Fossils. It is open from 12 noon to 4 p.m. Tuesday through Sunday, Memorial Day to Labor Day. The rest of the year it is open from 12 noon to 4 p.m. weekends.

In addition to "Old Main" on the Elgin Academy campus, there are four other individual properties and a historical district listed on the National Register of Historic Places. The individual listings are The First Universalist Church, 263 DuPage St.; Gifford Stone Cottage, 365 Prairie St.; Izzo-Pelton House, 214 State St.; and Elgin Milk Condensing Co., a structure bordered by Grove, North, Brook, and Water Sts. The Elgin Historic District is located on the east side of the city.

SOUTH ELGIN

Just south of Elgin, via IL 31, is SOUTH ELGIN (pop. 5,970), lying on both sides of the Fox River. The historical attraction here:

FOX RIVER TROLLEY MUSEUM, on IL 31, includes a three-mile ride on an 1896 electric railway. Also displayed are vintage railcars and railroad equipment. It is open 11 a.m. to 6 p.m. Sunday, mid-May through October, and 1 to 5 p.m. Saturday, July and August. Admission is free. There is a charge for the trolley rides.

THE DUNDEES

Back in Elgin and north, on IL 31, is WEST DUNDEE (pop. 3,551), once home of **Allan Pinkerton**, the famed detective.

Pinkerton arrived here in 1843 and eventually became Dundee's first cooper. His first cooperage was located on Third St., between Main St. and Oregon Ave. The second Pinkerton cooper shop was just west of the Wardle house which still stands at the

The Fox River Trolley Museum, South Elgin, features old railroad equipment.

This residence at 217 W. Main, West Dundee, was once the home of famed detective Allan Pinkerton.

southwest corner of Main and Sixth Sts. The house itself was a tavern serving the stage line to Galena. While cutting poles for barrel hoops he discovered a cache of counterfeit money which he turned over to the sheriff. The sheriff deputized him and asked him to keep an eye open for the counterfeiters in the event they returned for their loot. They did return and in the ensuing fight and investigation a band of lawbreakers were taken into custody.

An avid Abolitionist, Pinkerton helped to hide slaves in his shop. He was engaged to protect President-elect Abraham Lincoln and foiled an assassination attempt against him and then went on to organize the United States Secret Service. After the Civil War, Pinkerton established his detective agency and helped to round up many of the villians of the post-war years.

Many of the homes and buildings in Dundee are listed on the National Register of Historic Places. More than 60 buildings have been plaqued through the efforts of the Dundee Township Historical Society. A list of these may be obtained from the Society.

EAST DUNDEE is just across the Fox River from West Dundee. The historical attractions in the Dundees:

DUNDEE TOWNSHIP HISTORICAL SOCIETY, 426 Highland Ave., West Dundee, is housed in a 1925 parochial school building. It features exhibits and displays depicting local and area history including an Allan Pinkerton collection. It is listed on the National Register of Historic Places. It is open 2 to 4 p.m. Wednesday and Sunday and at other times by appointment. Admission is free.

HAEGER MUSEUM, 7 Maiden Lane, East Dundee, is part of the outlet store for Haeger Potteries, Inc., the world's largest art pottery. The exhibits show the evolution of the company as a brick and tile manufacturer in 1871 to its current position as a leading manufacturer of decorative accessories and lamps distributed throughout the world. The company operated a working factory at the 1933-34 Century of Progress Exposition in Chicago. It is open for free tours 8:30 a.m. to 5 p.m. Monday through Friday and 10 a.m. to 5 p.m. weekends and holidays. It is closed on New Year's Day, Easter, Thanksgiving Day, and Christmas.

Chapter 11
Touring Will County

Includes the following communities:
Frankfort
Joliet
Lockport
Plainfield
Peotone
Romeoville
Wilmington

The Museum Listings and Historic Sites
Fort Nonsense
Frankfort Area Historical Society
Historic Plank Toll Road
Illinois State Museum
Illinois & Michigan Canal National Heritage Corridor
Isle a la Cache Museum
John Lane Sr. Marker
Joliet Area Historical Society and Museum
Joliet Army Ammunition Plant
Joliet Correctional Center
Plainfield Historical Society Museum
Plainfield House
Rathje Dutch Mill
Stateville Correctional Center
Will County Historical Society
Wilmington Area Historical Society

Chapter 11
Touring Will County

JOLIET (pop. 77,956), county seat of Will County, is on the Des Plaines River and can be reached via I-55. It was settled in 1831, laid out in 1834, and incorporated as a village in 1837. The original name was Juliet and became Joliet in 1845 on the suggestion of President Martin Van Buren who spoke here. It is home of Stateville and Joliet Correctional Centers and the Joliet Army Ammunition Plant. The Army Ammunition Plant opened in 1940 north of Wilmington. It closed in 1975.

The prisons have always been a focal point in the community and home of the most infamous criminals in Illinois history. The prisons have played host to badmen such as killers **Richard Speck, William Heirens, Leopold and Loeb**; and kidnapper **Roger Touhy**. Richard Speck, born in 1941, forced his way into a nurses' residence at South Chicago Community Hospital, the night of July 13, 1966, and murdered eight student nurses. Heirens, born in 1929, was convicted of killing six-year old Suzanne Degnan, in 1946, and was sentenced to life imprisonment, never to be paroled. Nathan F. Leopold, Jr. (1906-71) and Richard A. Loeb (1907-36) kidnapped and murdered 14-year old Bobby Franks, son of a Chicago millionaire, May 22, 1924. Leopold reformed and was paroled in 1958. Loeb, who became an aggressive homosexual, was slashed to death in a shower by another prisoner in 1936. Roger Touhy, a Cook county bootlegger was convicted of kidnapping Jake "the Barber" Factor. He was released from prison in 1959.

The Jolict Center, or the "Old Prison," was opened in 1858 with 53 prisoners transferred here from the state's original prison in Alton. The state legislature authorized a new prison to be built five miles from Joliet. Work on Stateville, one of the better known prisons in the country, began in 1917 and, when completed in 1921, was the largest prison enclosure in the United States. Stateville officially opened March 9, 1925, and two days later began accepting inmates.

Prison labor was used for most of the construction work at Stateville and since the inmates were working in the open with no walls, more than 200 escaped.

One of the earliest escape attempts at Stateville came Febru-

The entrance and east wing of Joliet's "Old Prison," dating back to 1858.

A renovated roundhouse at Joliet's Stateville Prison.

Pictured here is John C. Houbolt, a native of Joliet, who is a world-famous aeronautical scientist. Another famous Jolietan is Mark Dragovan, a noted astronomer. Several other national and international figures claim Joliet as their hometown.

ary 22, 1931, when three inmates attempted to "go over the wall." **Joseph Norkiewicz**, 30, and **Julio Chileno**, 39, both confidence men, and **Alvin Kilmon, Jr.**, 33, a robber, were killed as they attempted their break. This incident became known among prisoners as **"The Washington Birthday Massacre."** Within a month of this episode, riots broke out at Joliet and Stateville, which led to the deaths of at least two inmates. **Henry "Midget" Ferneckes**, serving time for robbery, escaped from Joliet Prison on the afternoon of August 3, 1935. He was recaptured several months later and returned to Joliet. An escape attempt was thwarted at Stateville, September 14, 1939. The prison wall guards were drugged by an inmate to assist three inmates in their plan to "go over the wall," using a ladder. One of the guards, who did not drink his afternoon drugged coffee, spotted the trio and sounded the alarm. The escapees were seized as they were about to climb the ladder.

Among the Jolietans who gained national or international fame are the **Rev. Lawrence Martin Jenco**, **Mark Dragovan**, **John C. Houbolt**, **Lois Delander Lang**, and **A. L. "Al" Zimmerman**. Jenco was director of Relief Services in Beirut, Lebanon, when he was kidnapped, January 8, 1985, by pro-Iranian Shiite Moslems. Held hostage for 564 days, the clergyman was released July 26,

Noel's Livery Barn, S. Desplaines and Washington Sts., was a familiar sight to early day Jolietans.

Joliet Motor Co. once occupied this building downtown. It was burned during the race riots of April 1968.

1986. Dragovan, an astronomer, is one of three scientists investigating a powerful invisible source of gravity in the far reaches of the universe. Houbolt, an aeronautical scientist, is recognized world-wide for his work in dynamic load problems of aircraft and spacecraft, research on atmospheric turbulence, and expertise in the design of aircraft for turbulence encounter. Lois Delander was crowned Miss America of 1927, the first Illinoisan to become Miss America. Zimmerman was on a history-making 10,130-mile auto endurance African safari, known as the "Mediterranean-Capetown Rally," that began in December, 1950, and ended in February, 1951.

Several entertainers have their roots in Joliet. Among these are **James Beck**, TV actor with a long-standing role in "Dallas;" **James Downey**, a writer for "Saturday Night Live" and "David Letterman Show;" **Katherine Dunham**, choreographer and dancer; **Lucille Downey,** known professionally as Lucia Diano, an opera star in the 1930s; **Kathryn Hays**, TV actress with a long-standing role in "As The World Turns;" **Mercedes McCambridge**, who won the 1950 Oscar as best-supporting actress in the film, "All The King's Men;" **Larry Parks**, film actor, who starred as Al Jolson in "The Jolson Story;" **Lionel Richie**, song writer and vocalist; and **Audrey Totter**, 1940s movie star.

The Pulitzer Prize winning author, naturalist and photographer, **Edwin Way Teale** (1899-1980), was born in Joliet. He was the author of more than 30 books. Another Jolietan, **Robert "Bob" Upton** is another well-known author. Private detective Amos McGuffin is the main character in several of his novels. **Robert Novak**, who with Rowland Evans, writes the Evans-Novak syndicated column. He began his newspaper career as a part-time sports reporter for the Joliet newspaper. **Morton Kondrake** appears on TV with the McLaughlin Group and "This Week with David Brinkley." Both are graduates of Joliet high schools.

1st Sgt. Theodore Hyatt was the recipient of the Congressional Medal of Honor for heroism at the Battle of Vicksburg, May 22, 1863. Lt. Carl Lusic, a 1938 Joliet high school graduate, was the first fighter pilot to shoot down five enemy planes on a single mission. The 22-year old airman made history on May 8, 1944, in a raid on Berlin.

Col. Frederick Bartleson, of Joliet, organized the Union Grays, which evolved into the 20th and 100th Illinois Infantry Regiments during the Civil War. Bartleson participated in a number of campaigns during the war and died in Georgia in 1864. He is buried in Joliet's Oakwood Cemetery. Also buried here is **Sir William Van Horne**, the only Will Countian knighted by England. He was honored for his efforts as president of the Canadian Pacific Railroad.

Among the athletes from Joliet who earned a name in their sport: In baseball—**Sweetbreads Bailey, Jesse Barfield, Garland Buckeye, Bob Burke, Mark Grant, Bill Gullickson, Larry Gura, Bill Haller, Jack Hendricks, Ed Murphy, Jack Perconte, Jeff Reed, Bill Sudakis,** and **Eddie Spiezio.** In football—**Elmer "Tippy" Madarik, Tom Thayer,** and **Ernst "Pug" Rentner.** In basketball—**George Mikan**, in 1950 voted the greatest basketball player of the prior 50 years.

Several buildings in Joliet are listed on the National Register of Historic Places. These are Christ Episcopal Church, 75 W. Van Buren St.; Jacob H. Henry House, 20 S. Eastern Ave.; Joliet Municipal Airport hangar building, 4000 W. Jefferson St.; Joliet Township High School, 201 E. Jefferson St.; The Rialto Square Theater, 102 N. Chicago St.; Union Station, 50 E. Jefferson St.; the former U. S. Post Office, 150 N. Scott St.; and the former "silk stocking" ward, bounded by Washington Street, Union Avenue, Fourth Avenue, and Eastern Avenue.

The site of **Fort Nonsense** is marked at 320 N. Broadway. The fort, never used, was built in 1832 during the Black Hawk War. It become known as Fort Nonsense because it was built without making any provision for water in the event of an attack on the settlement.

A raised stone marker commemorates the plank toll road connecting Plainfield and Joliet. This marker is located on the south side of the Six Corners intersection, at Plainfield Road and Raynor Avenue in Joliet. The toll for use of the road was two cents per mile for a one-way trip.

The JOLIET AREA HISTORICAL SOCIETY AND MUSEUM, 17 E. Van Buren St., concentrates on local history. It is open 10 a.m. to 2 p.m. Saturday. Admission is free.

The ILLINOIS & MICHIGAN CANAL NATIONAL HERITAGE CORRIDOR VISITORS' CENTER is located at 30 N. Bluff St. It is open weekdays from 8 a.m. to 5 p.m. (For more information on I&M Canal National Heritage Corridor see Lockport listing in this section.)

PLAINFIELD

North on IL 59 is PLAINFIELD (pop. 3,777). It was settled in

1829 and incorporated in 1869. Originally it was called Walker's Grove. During the Black Hawk War, the home of Rev. Stephen Beggs was converted into an impromptu fort—Fort Beggs. At one time, 125 persons took refuge here for four days during the war.

Plainfield House, 503 Main St., was once known as Arnold's Tavern and served as a rest stop on the stage coach line from Chicago to Ottawa, started in 1834.

PLAINFIELD HISTORICAL SOCIETY MUSEUM features exhibits on local history, archaeology, military displays, and decorative arts. It is open 1 to 4 p.m. Saturdays. Admission is free.

LOCKPORT

Just north of Joliet, via IL 177, is LOCKPORT (pop. 9,192). The town was settled in 1830, laid out in 1837, and incorporated in 1853. Lockport got its name from Lock No. 1 on the 96-mile long Illinois & Michigan Canal opened in 1848. A few of the communities that sprang up and grew as a result of the Canal's openings were Lockport, Joliet, LaSalle, Marseilles, Morris and Ottawa. In recognition of the importance of the Canal to early-day transportation, it was designated a National Heritage Corridor in 1984. There are more than three dozen sites and structures in Lockport's historic district. The National Heritage Corridor includes more than 200 historic structures and districts.

The Gaylord Building, 200 W. 8th St., houses the I&M Canal Visitor Center.

John Lane, Sr. built the first steel plow in 1833. His first plow was not a success, but his second one, made a year later, was and several thousand were made and sold. He never patented it. A marker is located at the northeast corner of the intersection of Gougar Road and E. 7th Street in Lockport, commemorating Lane's invention.

Two major league baseball players were natives of Lockport, **Jim Donahue** and **Tom Haller**.

The first auto deaths occurred in Joliet in 1924 by a hit-and-run driver from Lockport. The driver smashed into seven pedestrians, killing a 32 year-old mother of six and a four year-old girl. The driver was identified, arrested and convicted of manslaughter. He was sentenced to one year to life in prison but was paroled after serving 11 months.

WILL COUNTY HISTORICAL SOCIETY, 803 S. State St., Lockport, devotes its efforts to local history. The Society administers the Pioneer Settlement, next to the Gaylord Building. The settlement's 15 structures and exhibits show what many midwestern towns were like in the mid-1800s. Up from the Pioneer Settlement is the I&M Canal Museum, also administered by the Society. The Society hours are from 1 to 4:30 p.m. daily. Admission is free.

ILLINOIS STATE MUSEUM (LOCKPORT GALLERY), 200 W. 8th St., 3rd floor, features fine, decorative, and industrial arts of Illinois. It is open 10 a.m. to 5 p.m. Tuesday through Sunday. Admission is free.

ROMEOVILLE

North of Joliet, via IL 53, is ROMEOVILLE (pop. 15,519), incorporated in 1895. It is home of the ISLE A LA CACHE MUSEUM, on 135th Street. The exhibits here captures the era of fur trading between the French and the Indians of the area. On weekends, the museum's staff dresses in authenic attire and presents demonstrations and programs. The museum, operated by the Will County Forest Preserve, is open daily, year-round, except Mondays. Admission is free.

WILMINGTON

Just south of Joliet is WILMINGTON (pop. 4,424). Wilmington, originally called Winchester, was one of the largest terminals in the Underground Railroad, a route to the North for escaped slaves. It was settled c. 1839 and incorporated in 1875.

The WILMINGTON AREA HISTORICAL SOCIETY is located at 100 N. Water St. It concentrates on the area's local history. It is open 1 to 4 p.m. weekends. Admission is free.

FRANKFORT

East of Joliet is FRANKFORT (pop. 4,357), just off US 45, home of FRANKFORT AREA HISTORICAL SOCIETY. Frankfort was founded in 1855 and incorporated in 1879. The museum is located on Kansas Street. It is open 1 to 4 p.m. Sundays, except holidays. Admission is free.

PEOTONE

In the southeast section of the county, off IL 50, is PEOTONE (pop. 2,832), settled in 1855 and incorporated in 1869. The Historical Society of Greater Peotone is currently restoring the H. A. Rathje Dutch Mill, on Corning Street, to house the Society's collections. The mill dates back to 1872.

Chapter 12
Miscellaneous

Listed in this chapter are 17 selected biographies and four other features. Also provided is a listing of Natural History and Nature Centers, public sculptures, and art museums and galleries.

Chapter 12
Miscellaneous

Established Memorial Day
Illinoisan John Alexander Logan (1826-1886) gained fame as a Union general and political leader. In 1862, he fought in all the Western campaigns under Gen. Ulysses S. Grant. He later distinguished himself at the siege of Vicksburg and served with Gen. William T. Sherman on the march through Georgia. Early in the war, he was appointed a colonel of an Illinois regiment. Logan was assigned as a major general of volunteers and a corps commander late in the war. He was a veteran of the Mexican War.

Logan was called "Black Jack" by his troops because of his dark complexion, eyes and hair. After the war he organized the Grand Army of the Republic, a veterans' organization. He is also credited with naming May 30, 1868, as the first Memorial Day.

Logan represented Illinois in the House of Representatives from 1859 to 1862 and from 1867 to 1871. He served in the U.S. Senate 1871 to 1877 and from 1879 until his death in 1886. He ran unsuccessfully for Vice President on the Republican ticket with James G. Blaine in 1884.

First Female State Representative
Lottie Holman O'Neill, from Downers Grove, was the first woman to be elected to the Illinois General Assembly. In 1922, two years after the 19th Amendment gave women the right to vote, DuPage County gave Illinois its first female state representative.

She was 44 years with two teenage boys when she entered politics. Mrs. O'Neill served in the Illinois House continuously from 1922 to 1963, except two years beginning in 1930. That year she lost her bid for the State Senate, and also failed in an attempt on the U. S. Senate. She returned to the Illinois House in 1932, and was elected to the State Senate in 1959, where she spent the rest of her career.

Mrs. O'Neill sponsored eight-hour workday legislation for women, and state aid to handicapped children. She was also a firm supporter of Prohibition. She was born in Barry, IL, November 7, 1878 and died in Downers Grove, February 17, 1967.

A 19th Century Exclusive Neighborhood

One of Chicago's exclusive neighborhoods in the late 19th century was Prairie Avenue. Among those in the "Prairie Avenue Set" were some of the wealthiest Chicago families.

Marshall Field built his $175,000 residence at 1905 Prairie Ave. in 1874.

Philip Armour, the meat packing king, lived at 2115 Prairie Ave.

George M. Pullman, the Pullman car millionaire, lived in a home built c. 1879 at 1729 Prairie Ave.

Two wealthy Chicagoans who chose other addresses were Louis H. Sullivan, the noted architect, and Potter Palmer, the entreprenuer. Sullivan resided at 4575 Lake Park Ave. from 1892 to 1897. Palmer built his home at 1350 North Shore Dr. in 1882. (This beautiful old home was demolished in 1950 to make way for an apartment complex.)

Ranked with Frank Lloyd Wright

Louis Henri Sullivan (1856-1924) ranks with Frank Lloyd Wright and Henry Hobson Richardson as one of America's greatest architects. He was a leader of the Chicago school of architecture.

Sullivan believed that a building should be *organic*, that is, it should be an expression of man's view of nature and society. He popularized the saying "form follows function."

He joined Dankmar Adler in 1879 and became a full partner with him in 1881. The Chicago Auditorium was built from 1886-89 and is believed to be Sullivan's first original design. The Carson Pirie Scott & Company store, at the corner of State and Madison Sts., was the last major building of Louis Sullivan and considered his masterpiece.

A Famous Muckraker

Upton Sinclair (1878-1968) became famous as a muckraker, a writer who exposed various social and political ills.

He gained national attention in 1906 with the release of "The Jungle," a brutally graphic novel of the Chicago stockyards. His book aroused public indignation and led to legislation creating some of the first U.S. pure food laws.

Sinclair used profits from this book to establish his short-lived socialist community, Helicon Home Colony, in Englewood, NJ. He was an active social and political reformer. He helped organize the American Civil Liberties Union (ACLU). He was an unsuccessful candidate for Congress three times and was defeated as the Democratic candidate for governor of California in 1934.

Sinclair received the Pulitzer Prize for fiction in 1943 for "Dragon's Teeth." The novel was one of the 11 in the Lanny Budd series written between 1940-53.

Dialogues with "Mr. Dooley"

Humorist Finley Peter Dunne (1867-1936), a native Chicagoan, gained fame as the creator of "Mr. Dooley," an Irish saloonkeeper. Dunne's dialogues with "Martin Dooley" were introduced in 1893 in the *Chicago Evening Post*.

As an incisive though humorous critic of American politics and society, "Mr. Dooley" gained nationwide notoriety for his jibes at the Spanish-American War. Dunne wrote a series of "Mr. Dooley" books beginning with "Mr. Dooley in Peace and War," released in 1898.

Dunne was an experienced Chicago journalist and wrote for the *Evening Post* and the *Times-Herald*. He served as editor-in-chief of the *Evening Post* during 1897-1900.

After leaving the newspaper business, Dunne worked for *McClure's Magazine* and *American Magazine*.

Clarence Darrow Biographer

Arthur Weinberg, who died in January 1989 at the age of 73, was the author of the 1957 best-seller, "Attorney for the Damned." The book was an anthology of the greatest summations of Clarence Darrow, the criminal and labor attorney perhaps best known for the 1925 John T. Scopes trial, in which he defended the right to teach evolution in Tennessee schools.

Weinberg and his wife, Lila, co-authored six other non-fiction works, including the 1980 biography "Clarence Darrow: A Sentimental Rebel," which received honors from the Friends of Literature and the Society of Midland Authors.

The couple's other books included, "The Muckrackers," one of the 1,780 books selected for the White House library by a committee of scholars during the Kennedy administration.

At the time of his death, the Weinbergs were in the midst of their eighth book and were consulting on two TV projects concerning Darrow's life.

The Weinbergs taught social history at DePaul University, including a class on "The Cases and Causes of Clarence Darrow."

Born and reared on the city's West Side, Weinberg received his bachelor's degree at Northwestern University. He was a self-styled "philosophical anarchist," a former president of a militant socialists' union and a social historian.

Served as Secretary of State

Edward R. Stettinius (1900-49), a Chicago native, served as U.S. Secretary of State in 1944-45.

Beginning in 1926, he held several executive positions in the General Motors Corporation. In 1938, he was named chairman of the board of U.S. Steel Corporation. He resigned in 1940 to join the National Defense Advisory Commission.

He served as priorities director in the Office of Production Management and as lend-lease administrator from 1941 to 1943. In 1943 he was appointed Undersecretary of State. In December 1944, he succeeded Cordell Hull as Secretary of State and served until June 1945.

Stettinius served as U.S. representative to the United Nations in 1945-46.

The First Baseball Commissioner

Kenesaw Mountain Landis (1866-1944) served as the first commissioner of professional baseball in 1920, after the 1919 scandal involving the Chicago White Sox and Cincinnati Reds. The White Sox "threw" the World Series.

Landis served many years as a judge of the U.S. District Court of Northern Illinois. He earned a reputation of fairness and captured national attention in 1907 when he fined the Standard Oil Company of Indiana $29,240,000 for accepting freight rebates.

Landis ruled baseball with an iron hand, and the game gained an unquestionable reputation for honesty. He was elected to the baseball Hall of Fame in 1944.

Softball Invented in Chicago

Softball was invented in Chicago in 1887 as an indoor game. At times it was called "indoor baseball," "mush ball," or "playground ball." Because it was also played by women it was also called "ladies' baseball" or "kitten ball." The name softball was given to the game in 1926.

The Amateur Softball Association of America, founded in 1934, governs the game and sponsors annual sectional and World series championships. The game gained in popularity as the result of a tournament held at the Chicago world's fair in 1933.

The ball is not soft. It is about 12 inches in diameter, three inches larger than a baseball. A softball infield is 60 feet square compared to a baseball infield of 90 feet. Until 1946 a softball team was made up of 10 players but since then a team consists of nine players on the field.

In softball the ball must be pitched underhand from 43 feet compared with 60.5 feet in baseball. A regulation game consists of seven innings.

The World's Busiest Airport

The world's busiest airport sprang from a 1,300 acre tract of government land called Orchard Field. From 1943-45 Orchard Field housed the Douglas Aircraft factory where military C-54's were built during World War II. In March, 1946, the City of Chicago obtained a large portion of that land. Its network of runways made it an attractive site for a second Chicago airport: Douglas Airport.

Douglas Airport was renamed Chicago O'Hare International Airport in honor of World War II naval hero, Lt. Edward "Butch" O'Hare, a native of St. Louis. The letters ORD still remain on tickets and baggage as an abbreviation for Orchard Field.

Scheduled airlines began using O'Hare, October 30, 1955. During the first year a total of 17 scheduled airlines served the airport. All scheduled airlines moved their operations from Midway Airport to O'Hare.

President John F. Kennedy officially dedicated Chicago O'Hare International Airport, March 23, 1963, calling it "...one of the wonders of the modern world."

Approximately 155,000 travelers pass through O'Hare every day. O'Hare Airport served almost 58 million passengers in 1987. An average of 110 aircraft arrive or depart each hour and nearly 800,000 aircraft arrive or depart each year. O'Hare serves over 50 airlines on a regular basis.

The O'Hare International Airport complex comprises nearly 7,000 acres. Arriving and departing aircraft are serviced by six runways, the longest being 13,000 feet.

Tours Offered At O'Hare

O'Hare International Airport's tour program offers tours of the airport at 10 and 11:30 a.m. weekdays. Children should be at least eight years of age. Groups must range in size from 20 to a maximum of 40 persons. Tours should be reserved at least one month in advance, although every effort will be made to accommodate reservations on shorter notice.

Any special arrangements, such as disabled or multi-lingual assistance should be requested when the reservation is made. Arrangements can be made by calling the Tour Guide office 8:30 a.m. to 4 p.m. weekdays at 686-2300.

Evanston's Namesake

The community of Evanston was named for John Evans (1814-97), an educator and real estate investor.

He was born in Waynesville, OH, and graduated from Lynn Medical College in 1838. He practiced medicine in Indiana and in 1845 was appointed the first superintendent of the state hospital for the insane which he had helped to establish.

Evans arrived in Chicago in 1848 to serve as a professor of obstetrics at Rush Medical School. He invested in real estate in what was to become Evanston. Here he helped found Northwestern University.

He served as governor of the Colorado Territory, 1862-65. Later he worked for the promotion of what became the University of Denver.

The Irreverent Country Musicians

Kenneth C. "Jethro" Burns and his longtime partner, Henry D. "Homer" Haynes, were irreverent country musician-comedians who drew heavily on their experiences in their hometown of Chicago for their acts. They played in Las Vegas and other major cities. They also appeared on the prominent network TV shows of Steve Allen and Johnny Carson.

Both were born in Knoxville, TN, and gained national attention as performers around 1950. The Homer & Jethro team took such pretty songs as "Doggie in the Window" and "Let Me Go, Lover" and transformed them into such ugly hits as "Hound Dog in the Winder" and "Let Me Go, Blubber."

From 1949 until the '60s, they starred on Chicago's "National Barn Dance." They recorded for several years with Chet Atkins as part of an instrumental group called the Nashville String Band. Burns began playing jazz in Chicago nightspots, recording for Chicago's Flying Fish Records with jazz violinist Joe Venuti and appearing with such artists as Pete Fountain and Steve Goodman. The partners settled in Chicago in 1949.

Haynes died of a heart attack in 1971; Burns died, February 4, 1989.

"Big Bill" Was Controversial Mayor

William Hale "Big Bill" Thompson (1869-1944) was born in Boston but moved to Chicago with his parents shortly after his birth. The feisty politician served as mayor of Chicago from 1915 to 1923 and from 1927 to 1931. He was tied to the underworld during his political career.

He controlled the city through a tightly-run political machine.

Thompson gained a reputation for his stands on national issues. During World War I, he opposed sending U.S. troops to fight against Germany and pro-war editorial writers labeled him "Kaiser Bill." In spite of his tirades against the country's involvement in the war, Chicago was among the leaders in subscriptions to Liberty Loan drives. A total of $772 million in bonds were sold here. In 1919, he ran on a "Freedom of Ireland" platform. In his 1927 campaign, he charged that British propaganda was creeping into U.S. textbook treatment of America's Revolutionary War.

He ran unsuccessfully for the U.S. Senate in 1918.

In 1931, Thompson was defeated by his Democratic challenger, Anton J. "Tony" Cermak. This defeat sent him into political oblivion.

Studs Lonigan Creator

James S. Farrell, born in Chicago in 1904, wrote the "Studs Lonigan" trilogy—"Young Lonigan," in 1932; "The Young Manhood of Studs Lonigan," in 1934; and "Judgment Day," in 1935.

His novels focused on life among the Irish Catholics on Chicago's South Side. His work was noted for the frankness of its language and its realism.

Following his Lonigan series, he wrote "A World I Never Made," in 1936; "No Star is Lost," in 1938; "Father and Son," in 1940; and "My Days of Anger," in 1943. He also wrote several volumes of short stories.

Farrell studied at the University of Chicago.

Arctic Explorer

Lincoln Ellsworth (1880-1951), a native Chicagoan, was an associate of Roald Amundsen in his arctic aviation ventures. In 1925, they flew in the dirigible *Norge N* from Spitsbergen over the North Pole to Alaska, where Ellsworth was acclaimed for saving the lives of two companions.

He was an observer in the 1931 flight of the *Graf Zeppelin* to Franz Josef Land and Northern Land.

In 1936, Ellsworth was the first to fly over the Antarctic from the Weddell Sea to the Ross Sea. He claimed 300,000 square miles (James W. Ellsworth Land) for the U.S. Three years later he flew over interior Antarctic from the Indian Ocean side. On this flight he claimed 81,000 square miles (American Highland) for the U.S.

Ellsworth, educated at Columbia and Yale, began as a surveyor and railroad construction engineer. Later he became a prospector and mining engineer in Canada.

His father left him a fortune, enabling him to become Amundsen's financial backer.

Famous American Sculptor

Lorado Taft (1860-1936), a native of Elmwood, IL, gained fame as a sculptor for his large memorials and fountains. Among these are the colossal "Black Hawk," overlooking the Rock River, near the community of Oregon, the "Fountain of the Great Lakes" and the "Fountain of Time," both in Chicago.

Taft studied art for three years at the Ecole des Beaux Arts in Paris after his graduation from the University of Illinois. In 1886, he became an instructor in the Art Institute of Chicago where he exerted a strong influence over young Western sculptors. He later taught at the University of Illinois.

After decorative sculptures for the horticulture building at the Columbian Exposition in Chicago in 1893, he produced portrait work, military monuments, and groups such as "Solitude of the Soul" and "The Blind," at the Art Institute of Chicago.

Among some of his other major works are the Washington monument in Seattle, the "Thatcher Memorial Fountain" in Denver, and the "Columbus Memorial Fountain" in Washington, D.C.

The Stone Brothers

Melvin J. Stone (1848-1929), born in Hudson, IL, was one of the founders of the *Daily News* in 1876, the first Chicago penny paper. In 1881, he was one of the founders of the *Morning News*, later called the *Record*.

Stone was named general manager of the reorganized Associated Press in 1893, and under his direction it became one of the great news agencies. He retired in 1921.

His brother, Ormond (1847-1933), born in Pekin, IL, graduated from the University of Chicago and became a noted astronomer. In 1884, he founded the *Annals of Mathematics* and edited it for several years.

Stone observed the 1869 solar eclipse in Iowa and led eclipse expeditions in 1878 and 1900. He wrote numerous papers for astronomical and mathematical journals.

Noted Editorial Cartoonist

Herbert L. Block, the noted editorial cartoonist who signed his work as Herblock, was born in Chicago in 1909. He became famous in the 1950s for his cartoons attacking Senator Joseph R. McCarthy and won the Pulitzer prize for cartooning in 1942 and in 1954.

He became an editorial cartoonist for the *Chicago Daily News* in 1929. Herblock joined the Newspaper Enterprise Association as a syndicated cartoonist in 1933. He served in the Army during World War II and joined the *Washington Post* in 1946. Later he joined the Field Newspaper Syndicate.

Block studied at Lake Forest College and the Art Institute of Chicago before joining the *Daily News*. Several books of Herblock's cartoons have been published including "The Herblock Book" (1952), "Herblock's Here and Now" (1955), and "Herblock Special Report" (1974).

Favorite of Movie-Goers

Gloria Swanson, born in Chicago, March 27, 1899, made her first appearance in the movies in a bit part for the old Chicago Essanay Studios in 1914. After a year at Essanay Studios she went to Hollywood.

A month after her arrival on the West Coast, she was playing leading roles in domestic comedies for Keystone Studios. Her big break came at the age of 19 when she was discovered by Cecil B. DeMille. He gave her the part of a sophisticated woman in the 1918 film, "Don't Change Your Husband." This was the first of the opulent, lavish productions which made Miss Swanson a favorite of the nation's movie-goers.

DeMille's judgment of the girl was more than justified. Her looks and photogenic qualities were ideal for his pictures. She wore clothes with verve and chic. Her well-defined features, retrousse nose, light eyes and flashing teeth made her stand apart from the uniformly sweet-faced ingenues.

She made six pictures with DeMille including "For Better For Worse," "Male and Female," and "Why Change Your Life."

Among some of her great films were: "The Great Moment," "Her Husband's Trademark," "The Gilded Cage," "My American Wife," "Prodigal Daughter," "Bluebeard's Eighth Wife," "Wages of Virtue," "Untamed Lady," "Fine Manners," and "Humming Bird."

Miss Swanson, who married five times, appeared in 56 films. She died April 4, 1983.

Natural History and Nature Centers

This section includes Nature Centers not listed elsewhere. These are listed in alphabetical order.

CRABTREE NATURE CENTER, Palatine Rd., Barrington. Hours: 9 a.m. to 4:30 p.m. Monday through Thursday; 9 a.m. to 5 p.m. weekends and holidays in the summer months. Winter schedule: 9 a.m. to 4 p.m. daily. Admission is free.

FULLERSBURG WOODS NATURE CENTER, 3609 Spring Rd., Oak Brook. Hours: 9 a.m. to 5 p.m. daily (Environmental Center). Closed during weekends and holidays. Admission is free.

WALTER E. HELLER NATURE PARK AND INTERPRETIVE CENTER, 2821 Ridge Rd., Highland Park. Hours: 8:30 a.m. to 5 p.m. Monday through Saturday; 12 noon to 4 p.m. Sunday. Closed on holidays. Admission is free.

JURICA NATURAL HISTORY MUSEUM, Illinois Benedictine College, 5700 College Rd., Lisle. Hours: 12 noon to 4 p.m. Wednesday and Sunday; special tours by appointment. Admission is free.

LITTLE RED SCHOOLHOUSE NATURE CENTER, Willow Springs Rd. at 104th Ave., Willow Springs. Hours: 9 a.m. to 4:30 p.m. Monday through Thursday; 9 a.m. to 5 p.m. weekends and holidays except Friday, Thanksgiving, Christmas, and New Year's. Admission is free.

NORTH PARK VILLAGE NATURE CENTER, 5801 N. Pulaski Rd., Chicago. Hours: 11 a.m. to 3 p.m. daily. Closed on holidays. Admission is free.

RIVER TRAIL NATURE CENTER, Milwaukee Ave., Northbrook. Hours: 9 a.m. to 4:30 p.m. Monday through Thursday; 9 a.m. to 5 p.m. weekends and holidays during the summer months. Winter schedule: 9 a.m. to 4 p.m. daily except Friday, Thanksgiving, Christmas, and New Year's. Admission is free.

EDWARD L. RYERSON CONSERVATION AREA, 21950 N. Riverwoods Rd., Deerfield. Hours: 8:30 a.m. to 5 p.m. daily. Admission is free.

SAND RIDGE NATURE CENTER, Paxton Ave., South Holland. Hours: 9 a.m. to 4:30 p.m. Monday through Thursday; 9 a.m. to 5 p.m. weekends and holidays during the summer months. Winter schedule: 9 a.m. to 4 p.m. daily except Friday, Thanksgiving, Christmas, and New Year's. Admission is free.

TRAILSIDE MUSEUM OF NATURAL HISTORY, 738 Thatcher Ave., River Forest. Hours: 10 a.m. to 12 noon and 1 to 4 p.m. daily. Closed Thursday, Thanksgiving, Christmas, and New Year's. Admission is free.

WILLOWBROOK WILDLIFE HAVEN, Willowbrook Forest Preserve, Park Blvd. between Roosevelt and Butterfield Rds., Glen Ellyn. Hours: 9 a.m. to 5 p.m. daily except Thanksgiving, Christmas, and New Year's. Admission is free.

Public Sculptures
Chicagoland is noted for its sculpture in public places.
IN CHICAGO'S CENTRAL BUSINESS DISTRICT
Batcolumn (1977) by Claes Oldenberg, 600 W. Madison St., on the Social Security Administration Building Plaza.

Being Born (1982) by Virginio Ferrari, State and Washington Sts., on State Street Mall.

Ceres (1930) by John Storrs, 141 W. Jackson Blvd at Jackson St., at the Board of Trade Building.

Chicago Picasso (1967) by Pablo Picasso, Washington and Dearborn Sts., on the Daley Civic Center Plaza.

Dawn Shadows (1983) by Louise Nevelson, Madison and Wells Sts., on Madison Plaza.

Flamingo (1974) by Alexander Calder, Adams and Dearborn Sts., on the Federal Center Plaza.

The Four Seasons (1974) by Marc Chagall, Monroe and Dearborn Sts., on the First National Bank Plaza.

George Washington-Robert Morris-Haym Solomon Memorial Monument (1941) by Lorado Taft, Wacker Dr. and Wabash Ave., on Heald Square.

Merchandise Mart Hall of Fame (1953) by Minna Harkavy, Milton Horn, Lewis Iselin, Henry Rox, and Charles Umlauf, at the main entrance of Merchandise Mart, on the Chicago River between Wells and Orleans St.

Miro's Chicago (1981) by Joan Miro, 69 W. Washington St., on the Brunswick Building Plaza.

Monument with Standing Beastd (1984) by Jean Dubuffet, Randolph and Clark Sts., on the State of Illinois Building Plaza.

Sounding Sculpture by Harry Bertoia (1975), 200 E. Randolph Sts., on the Amoco Building Plaza.
ELSEWHERE IN CHICAGO
Abraham Lincoln (1887) by Augustus Saint-Gaudens, in Lincoln Park, North Ave. near Clark St.

Bison by Edward Kemeys, in Humboldt Park, near Sacramento Blvd. and Division St.

Chicago Stock Exchange Arch (1893) by Adler and Sullivan, at the east entrance of the Art Institute of Chicago.

Clarence Buckingham Fountain (1927) by Bennett, Parsons & Frost, in Grant Park.

Elks National Memorial Sculpture (1926) by Gerome Brush, Laura Gardin Fraser, and Adolph Alexander Weinman, 2750 N. Lakeview Ave., at the Elks National Memorial and Headquarters Building.

The Eugene Field Memorial (1922) by Edward McCartan (1922), in Lincoln Park (east of the Small Animal House at the zoo).

The Fountain of the Great Lakes (1913) by Lorado Taft, the south wing of the Art Institute of Chicago.

Fountain of Time (1922) by Lorado Taft, in Washington Park.

From Here to There (1975) by Richard Hunt, 43rd St. and Cottage Grove Ave., Martin Luther King Community Service Center.

General John Logan Memorial (1897) by Augustus Saint-Gaudens and Alexander Phimister Proctor, in Grant Park.

I Will (1981) by Ellsworth Kelly, in Lincoln Park, Fullerton and Ave. and Cannon Dr.

Illinois Centennial Memorial Column (1918) by Evelyn Beatrice Longman and Henry Bacon, in Logan Square, Logan Blvd. and Milwaukee Ave.

In Celebration of the 200th Anniversary of the Founding of the Republic (1976) by Isamu Noguchi, the east facade of the Art Institute of Chicago.

Independence Square (1902) by Charles J. Mulligan, in Independence Square, Douglas and Independence Blvds.

Indians (1928) by Ivan Mestrovic, in Grant Park.

Lions (1894) by Edward Kemeys, at the west entrance of the Art Institute of Chicago.

Monument to Johann Wolfgang von Goethe (1913) by Herman Hahn, in Lincoln Park.

Nicholas Copernicus (original in 1823, reproduced in 1973) by Bertel Thorvaldsen and Bronislaw Koniuszy, in Burnham Park, Solidarity Dr. to Adler Planetarium.

Nuclear Energy (1967) by Henry Moore, at the University of Chicago, Ellis Ave. between 56th and 57th Sts.

The Republic (1918) by Daniel Chester French, in Jackson Park.

The Spirit of DuSable Sculpture Garden (1963 and 1977) by Robert Jones, Ausbra Ford, Geraldine McCullough, Jill Parker, Ramon Bertell Price, and Lawrence E. Taylor, DuSable Museum of African American History, in Washington Park.

Stephen A. Douglas Tomb and Memorial (1881) by Leonard Wells Volk, in Douglas Tomb State Memorial Park, 35th St. east of Cottage Grove Ave.

Sundial (1980) by Henry Moore, in Burnham Park, Solidarity Dr.

Thaddeus Kosciuszko Memorial (1904) by Kasimir Chodzinski, in Burnham Park, Solidarity Dr.

Thomas Garrigue Masaryk Memorial (1941) by Albin Polasek, near Jackson Park.

Ulysses S. Grant Memorial (1891) by Louis T. Rebisso, in Lincoln Park.

Untitled Light Sculpture (1981) by Hyong Nam Ahn, at McCormick Place Donnelley Hall Plaza, 23rd St. and Dr. Martin Luther King, Jr. Dr.

Victory, World War I Black Soldiers' Memorial (1927) by Leonard Crunelle, at 35th St. and Dr. Martin Luther King, Jr. Dr.

SCULPTURES IN THE SUBURBS

The Bather (1975) by Pablo Picasso, in Gould Center, Golf Rd., Rolling Meadows.

Large Two Forms (1969) by Henry Moore, in Gould Center, Golf Rd., Rolling Meadows.

Nathan Manilow Sculpture Park (started in 1976) by Mark di Suvero, Charles Ginnever, John Henry, Jene Highstein, Richard Hunt, Jerald Jacquard, Mary Miss, John Payne, Jerry Peart, Martin Puryear, and Edvins Strautmanis, at Governors State University, University Park.

Vita (1969) by Virginio Ferrari, at Loyola University Medical Center, 2160 S. 1st Ave., Maywood.

Art Museums and Galleries

This section includes art museums and galleries not listed elsewhere. These are listed in alphabetical order.

MARY AND LEIGH BLOCK GALLERY, Northwestern University, 1967 Sheridan Rd., Evanston. Hours: 10:30 a.m. to 4:30 p.m. Tuesday through Saturday; 12 noon to 5 p.m. Sunday. Admission is free.

BEVERLY ART CENTER, 2153 W. 111th St., Chicago. Hours: 8 a.m. to 6 p.m. weekdays; 10 a.m. to 2 p.m. Saturday; and 1 to 4 p.m. Sunday. Admission is free.

CHICAGO AND A. MONTGOMERY WARD GALLERIES, University of Illinois Circle Campus, Chicago Circle Center Programs Dept., 750 S. Halsted St., Chicago. Hours at Chicago Gallery: 10 a.m. to 5 p.m. weekdays. Hours at Ward Gallery: 11 a.m. to 6 p.m. weekdays, 1 to 5 p.m. Saturday. Admission is free.

COUNTRYSIDE ART CENTER, 408 N. Vail Ave., Arlington Heights. Hours: 1 to 5 p.m. Tuesday through Sunday. Admission is free.

MARTIN D'ARCY GALLERY OF ART, Loyola University, 6525 N. Sheridan Rd., Chicago. Hours: 12 noon to 4 p.m. Monday, Wednesday, and Friday; 12 noon to 4 p.m. Tuesday and Thursday; 6:30 p.m. to 9:30 p.m. Sunday. Closed when school is not in session. Admission is free.

DEERPATH GALLERY, 1 Market Square Ct., Lake Forest. Hours: 10 a.m. to 4 p.m. Monday through Saturday. Admission is free.

EVANSTON ART CENTER, 2603 Sheridan Rd., Evanston. Hours: 10 a.m. to 4 p.m. Monday, Tuesday, Wednesday, Friday, and Saturday; 10 a.m. to 4 p.m. and 7 to 10 p.m. Thursday; and 2 to 5 p.m. Sunday. Donations are accepted.

HYDE PARK ART CENTER, 1701 E. 53rd St., Chicago. Hours: 11 a.m. to 5 p.m. Tuesday through Saturday. Admission is free.

NORTH SHORE ART LEAGUE, 620 Lincoln Ave., Winnetka. Hours: 9 a.m. to 10 p.m. Monday through Saturday. Admission is free.

SISTER GUALA O'CONNOR ART GALLERY, Rosary College, 7900 W. Division St., River Forest. Hours: 12 noon to 4 p.m. weekdays. Admission is free.

PARK FOREST ART CENTER, 410 Lakewood, Park Forest. Hours: 1 to 3 p.m. Monday, Tuesday, Thursday, and Friday; 7:30 to 9 p.m. Monday and Thursday; 10 a.m. to 3 p.m. Sunday. Admission is free.

REICHER GALLERY, Barat College, 700 Westleigh Rd., Lake Forest. Hours: 12 noon to 4 p.m. Monday through Saturday. Admission is free.

RENAISSANCE SOCIETY, University of Chicago, 5811 S. Ellis Ave., Chicago. Hours: 10 a.m. to 4 p.m. Tuesday through Friday, and 12 noon to 4 p.m. weekends, October through June. Closed on holidays. Admission is free.

DAVID AND ALFRED SMART GALLERY, University of Chicago, 5550 S. Greenwood Ave., Chicago. Hours: 10 a.m. to 4 p.m. Tuesday through Saturday; 12 noon to 4 p.m. Sunday. Closed holidays and month of September. Admission is free.

SONNENSCHEIN GALLERY, Lake Forest College, E. Deerpath and N. Sheridan Rds., Lake Forest. Hours: 3 to 5 p.m. weekdays; 2 to 5 p.m. weekends. Admission is free.

SOUTH SIDE COMMUNITY ART CENTER, 3831 S. Michigan Ave., Chicago. Hours: 1 to 7 p.m. Tuesday through Friday; 1 to 5 p.m. weekends. Admission is free.

STATE OF ILLINOIS ART GALLERY, State of Illinois Building, 100 W. Randolph St., Chicago. Hours: 10 a.m. to 6 p.m. weekdays. Admission is free.

SUBURBAN FINE ARTS CENTER, 777 Central Ave., Highland Park. Hours: 9:30 a.m. to 4 p.m. weekdays. Admission is free.

INDEX

Addison 153, 154
Addams, Jane 94
Ade, George 49
Adler, Danknar 224, 235
Adler, Max 73
Adler Planetarium 60, 70, 73, 236
Ahn, Hyong Nam 236
Agar, John 48
Aiello, Andrew 58
Aiello, Antonio 58
Aiello, Dominick 58
Aiello, Joseph 58
Albright Gallery of Painting and Sculpture 151, 152
Algren, Nelson 49
Allex, Cpl. Jake 47
Amateur Softball Association of America 227
Amatuna, Sam "Smoots" 57
American Civil Liberties Union (ACLU) 225
American Highland 231
American League 13
American Magazine 225
American Police Center and Museum 96, 97, 98
American Railway Union 36
American Steel and Wire Company 197
Amoco Oil Building 35, 68
Amos 'n' Andy 41
Amundsen, Roald 231
Anderson, 1st Sgt. Johannes S. 47
Anderson, Herbert 43
Anselmi, Albert 57
AntiFact Center (Spertus Museum) 81
Antique Hub of Northern Illinois 184
Antrim, Harry 48
Applebee House 119
Archange 111
Ardmore Avenue Station 141
Arlington Heights 114, 237
Arlington Heights Historical Museum 114
Armour, Philip 224
Army of the Potomac 202
Art Institute of Chicago 7, 79, 176, 235, 236
Atcher, Robert O. 122
Atkins, Chet 229
Augusta 29
Aurora 8, 151, 189, 190

Aurora College 8
Aurora Fire Museum 191
Aurora Historical Museum 189, 190
Aurora Hotel 192
Aurora Police Department Museum 191

Bacon, Henry 236
Baha'i House of Worship 111, 112
Bailey, Sweetbreads 218
Baker, Edward John 199
Baker Hotel 202
Balbo, Italo 42
Balzekas Museum of Lithuanian Culture 92
Bang, Justice 172
Bangs Lake 172
Banta House 114
Barat College 8, 238
Barfield, Jesse 218
Barrington 119, 234
Barrington Area Historical Society Museum 119, 121
Barry, Dave 14
Bartleson, Col. Frederick 217
Bartlett, 122
Bartlett Historical Museum 118, 122
Bartlett, Luther 122
Bassett, Arthur "Rip" 50
Batavia 151, 189, 194
Batavia Depot Museum 193, 195
Batcolumn 235
Bates, Granville 48
The Bather 237
Battle of Mine Creek 202
Beaubien, Marc 149
Beaubien, Jean Baptist 149
Beck, James 217
The Beehive 154
Being Born 235
Belcastro, James 58
Bell, Rex 48
Bellevue Place 194, 195
Bellow, Samuel 49
Bennett, Dave 199
Bennett, Parson & Frost 235
Benny, Jack 159, 160
Bensenville 154
Bensenville Historical Society 154
Berardi, Tony 64
Bergen, Edgar 48
Berman, Shelley 177

Berry, John 37
Berwyn 107
Bertoia, Harry 235
Bethany Theological Seminary 7
Beveridge, Col. John L. 202
Beverly Art Center 237
Bigelow, WT1/c Elmer C. 180
Biograph Theatre 60
Bishop, Wallace Henry "Bish" 50
Bison 235
Blackberry Historical Farm—Village 194
Black Hand 58
Black Hawk War 24
Blaine, James G. 223
Block, Herbert L. 232
Bloody Angelo 57
Bloomingdale 156
Bloomingdale Park District Museum 156
Blue Island 126
Blue Island Historical Society 126
Blue Island Museum 126
Mr. Bluebeard 28
Bondi, Beulah 48
Bonfield, Capt. John 31, 34
Boone, Mayor Levi D. 26
Bosley, Tom 177
"Bottles," Ralph J. 55
Bowen Park Haines Farmhouse 157, 158
Boxleitner, Bruce 115, 183, 184
Bradbury, Ray 159, 161
Braddock, James J. 14
Bradford Museum of Collector's Plates 113
Breasted, James Henry 90, 147
Bridgeport 11
Brooks, Gwendolyn 49
Brothers, Leo 56
"Brown Bomber" 14
Brush, Gerome 235
Bryan, Charles P. 141
Bryan, Thomas Barber 141
Buck, Fred 162
Buckeye, Garland 218
Buckingham Fountain 67, 68, 235
Buffalo Grove 114
Buffalo Grove Historical Society 114
Burke, Bob 218
Burnham, Daniel H. 13, 71
Burnham Park 236
Burns, Kenneth C. "Jethro" 229
Burroughs, Margaret and Charles 84
Butler, Frank O. 145

Cabrini-Green Housing Project 11
Calder, Alexander 235
Calumet Country Club 22
Camp Douglas 27, 28, 29
Camp Kane 195, 202
Canadian Pacific Railroad 218
Cantigny 135, 136, 137
Canzoneri, Tony 14
Capone, Al "Scarface" 55, 56, 57, 58, 59, 62, 60, 63, 64, 98
Car Barn Bandits 38
Carol Stream 143
Carol Sue 48
Carman, Doreston, Jr. 164
Carpentersville 189
Carson Pirie Scott & Company 224
Cavalier, Robert 21
Century of Progress Exposition 42
Ceres 235
Cermak, Mayor Anton J. "Tony" 42, 230
Cernan, Eugene A. (Astronaut) 105
Cernan Earth and Space Center 105, 106
Chadron (Nebraska) to Chicago Cowboy Horse Race 37
Chagall, Marc 225
Champion, Gower 197
Chaplin, Charlie 49
Chekagon 21
Chicago 11, 13, 21, 24, 34, 38, 41, 42, 43, 49, 50, 51, 55, 58, 64, 67, 70, 78, 79, 84, 85, 88, 105, 178, 164, 172, 189, 224, 225, 226, 227, 228, 229, 230, 232, 233, 234, 235, 237, 238
Chicago Academy of Sciences 88
Chicago Architecture Foundation 90
Chicago Auditorium 224
Chicago and A. Montgomery Ward Galleries 237
Chicago Bears 11, 13, 15, 17
Chicago Black Hawks 11, 15
Chicago Board of Trade 11, 81
Chicago Bulls 11, 15
Chicago Cardinals 17
Chicago Circle 7
Chicago Cubs 11, 15
Chicago Daily News 13, 31
Chicago Democrat 24
Chicago Historical Society 22
Chicago Historical Society Museum 88
Chicago Flying Fish Records 229
Chicago Evening Post 225
Chicago Maritime Museum 73

240

Chicago Mercantile Exchange 81
Chicago O'Hare International Airport 45, 46, 228
Chicago Picasso 39, 235
Chicago Post Office 11
Chicago River 21, 35, 38
Chicago Sanitary and Ship Canal 11, 38
Chicago School of Architecture 224
Chicago Stadium 11, 14
Chicago State University 7
Chicago Stock Exchange Arch 235
Chicago Sun 31
Chicago Suntimes 31
Chicago Times-Herald 37
Chicago Tribune 13, 55, 131 133, 135, 136
Chicago-Tribune-New York News Syndicate 178
Chicago White Sox 13, 227
Chicago's famed Water Tower 30
Chileno, Julio 215
Chinatown 11
Chodzinski, Kasimir 236
Christ Episcopal Church 218
Christian Catholic Church 162
Church of the Big and Little Woods 151
Cicero 55, 57
Cincinnati Reds 227
Clark, James 60
Clarke, Henry B. 90
Clary, Charles 199
Cleveland, President Grover 36
Cody, Col. William F. "Buffalo Bill" 37
Colvin House 141
Coldwell, Albert W. "Happy" 50
College of Pacific 14
College of St. Francis 8
Colosimo, Big Jim 55
Columbia College 7, 79
Comiskey, Charles 15
Comiskey Park 13
Concordia Teachers College 7
Confederate Mound Memorial 28
Congressional Medal of Honor 46, 47
Conley Prints 22
Conley, Walter 22, 23
Construction Battalion Unit 401 168
Conzelman, Jim 18
Cook, Andrew C. 172
Cook, Andrew, Museum 172, 174
Cook, Ansel B. 171, 172
Cook County 7, 21, 114, 131

Cook County Democratic organization 42
Cook County Jail 37
Cook, Daniel P. 7
Coolidge, President Calvin 107
Coonley House 103
Copernicus Cultural and Civic Center 92
Copley Mansion 192
Correll, Charles 41
Cosley Animal Farm and Museum 141
Countryside Art Center 237
Count's Home 184
Crabtree Nature Center 234
Cronan, B. M. Willie 47
Crosby, Israel 50
Crowley, Samuel P. 63
Crown, Robert, Center for Health Education 147
Crunelle, Leonard 237
Crystal Lake 8, 115, 183, 184, 185, 186
Cubs (see Chicago Cubs)
Curie, Marie 88
Curtis, Alan 48
Curtiss-Reynolds airport 122
Czechoslovak Heritage Museum 107

D'Albrook, Sidney 48
Daily News 232
Daily Times 31
Daily Tribune 24
Daley, Mayor Richard J. 42
Daley, Richard J., Civic Center Plaza 39
Dalton, Dorothy 48
Darro, Frank 48
Darrow, Clarence 13, 226
Dawes, Vice President Charles Gates 107, 108
Dawn Shadows 235
Debs, Eugene V. 13, 36, 177
Deerfield 170, 234
Deerfield Historical Museum 170
Deerpath Gallery 237
Degnan, Suzanne 37
DeHaven, Carter 48
Delander, Lois 217
DeMille, Cecil B. 233
Democratic national convention 41, 42
Dempsey, Jack 14
Deneen, Sen. Charles S. 58
DePalma, Ralph 204
DePaul University 7
Des Plaines 115

241

Des Plaines Historical Society Museum 116
Detroit Mirror 180
diSuvero, Mark 237
Diano, Lucia 217
Dickinson Hotel 159
Dillinger, John 55, 61, 60, 63
Dole, Charles S. 183, 185
Dole Mansion 183, 185
Donahue, Jim 219
Donlea/Kincaid House 119, 121
Dos Passos, John 13
Douglas Airport 228
Douglas, Senator Stephen A. 25, 26
Douglas, Stephen A., Tomb and Memorial 29
Douglas Tomb State Historical Site 25
Douglas Tomb State Memorial Park 29, 236
Dowie, John Alexander 162
Downers Grove 147, 148, 223
Downers Grove Historical Museum 147
Downer, Pierce 147
Downey, James 217
Downey, Lucille 217
Downtown Chicago 11
Dragovan, Mark 215, 217
Drucci, Schemer 56, 57
Drucci, Vincent 56
Dubuffet, Jean 235
Dundee Township Historical Society 210
"Dunham Castle" 155, 156, 199
Dunham, Katherine 217
Dunham, Mark W. 156, 199
Dunham-Hunt Museum 199, 200
Dunne, Finley Peter 225
DuPage County 7, 131, 133, 135, 223
DuPage County Historical Museum 138, 140
DuPage Heritage Gallery 131, 132, 133, 134
Durant-Peterson House 201, 202
Durbahn, Walt, Tool Museum 170
Duryea, Frank 38
Duryea Motor Wagon 38
duSable, Jean Baptiste Point 21
DuSable Museum of African American History 84, 87, 236

East Dundee 189, 210
Eastland 38
Edison Thomas 183
Eisenhower Expressway 11
Elgin 8, 203, 204, 205, 206, 207
Elgin Academy 204, 205, 207
Elgin Area Convention and Visitors Bureau 204
Elgin Area Historical Museum 205, 206
Elgin Automobile Road Race Association 204
Elgin Historic District 207
Elgin Milk Condensing Co. 207
Elgin National Road Race 204, 206
Elgin Public Museum 207
Eliot, T. S. 50
Elk Grove Village 115, 119
Elk Grove Historical Society 115, 117
Elks (Benevolent and Protective Order of Elks) 41
Elks National Memorial Building 41
Elks National Memorial Sculpture 235
Ellsworth, Col. Elmer E. 29
Ellsworth, James W., land 229
Ellsworth, Lincoln 230
Elmhurst 141
Elmhurst College 7
Elmhurst Historical Museum 141
Elmwood 231
Elmwood Park 106
Engel, George 34
Esposito, Diamond Joe 58
Essanay Studios 40, 49, 233
Eugene Field Memorial 235
Evans, John 229
Evans, Rowland 217
Evanston 38, 107, 110, 113, 229, 237
Evanston Art Center 237
Evanston College for Ladies 36
Evanston Historical Society 107 108
The Evening American 64
Evatt, Gail 107

Fabyan, Col. George 196, 197
Fabyan Villa Museum 196, 197
Factor, Jake "the Barber" 63
Fardy, Cpl. John P. 47
Farley, Dot 48
Farmhouse Museum 115, 117
Farnsworth, John Franklin 202
Farrell, James S. 230
Farrell, James T. 49
Farson, John 106
Farson-Mills House 106
Fenwick, Irene 48
Fermi, Dr. Enrico 43, 151
Fermi National Accelerator Laboratory 151, 194
Ferneckes, Henry "Midget" 215
Ferrari, Virginio 235, 237

242

Fibber McGee and Molly 41
Field, Ben 34
Field, Marshall 26, 31, 67, 71, 223
Field, Marshall III 31
Field, Marshall IV 31
Field, Marshall V 31
Field Museum of National History 31, 67, 69, 74, 75, 76, 77
Fielden, Samuel 34
15th U.S. Cavalry 165
1st (The Big Red One) Division Museum 135, 136, 137
First Universalist Church 207
Fischer, Adolph 34
Fisher, Lt. John H. 46
Flamingo 235
Flynn, Bernadine 41
Ford, Ausbra 236
Fort Beggs 219
Fort Dearborn 21, 24
Fort Douglas 168
Fort Nonsense 218
Fort Payne 149
Fort Sheridan 165, 166, 168
Fort Sheridan Museum 165, 166, 170
Fort Sheridan Tower 167
Foster, Frank 60
Foster, Susanna 48
Fountain of the Great Lakes 236
Fountain of Time 236
Fountain, Pete 229
Four Deuces Brothel 56
Four Seasons 235
Fox River Trolley Museum 207, 208
Franey, William "Billy" 48
Frankfort 220
Frankfort Area Historical Society 220
Franks, Bobby 13, 37, 213
Fraser, Laura Gardin 235
Freemeyer, Pvt. Christopher 46
French, Daniel Chester 236
From Here to There 236
Frost, Robert 50
Fuller, Benjamin 147
Fullersburg Woods Nature Center 234

GAR (Grand Army of the Republic) Memorial and Veteran's Military Museum 190, 191, 192
"Galloping Ghost" 17
Galluccio, Frank 55
Garfield Farm Museum 197
Garner, Jack 42
Gary, Judge Elbert H. 131, 134
Gates, John Warne "Bet-A-Million" 131, 133, 199

Gaylord Building 219, 220
General John Logan Memorial 236
Geneva 8, 151, 189, 196, 197
Geneva Historical Society Museum 193, 197
Gennas, Jim 57
Gennas, Pete 57
Gennas, Sam 57
George Washington-Robert Morris-Haym Solomon Memorial Monument 235
Germantown Rockaway Carriage 166
Gerson, Noel 49
Gerstung, T/Sgt. Robert E. 47
Gibson, T/5 Eric G. 47
Gifford Stone Cottage 207
Gillis, Henel 63
Gillis, Lester M. 63
Ginnever, Charles 237
Glen Ellyn 138 139, 143, 144, 236
Glencoe 113
Glencoe Historical Museum 113
Glenview 122, 164
Glenview Historical Museum 123, 125
Glenview Naval Air Station 122, 123
Glessner house 92
Glessner, John J. 90
Glidden, Joseph 197
Glos, Village President Henry 141
Goettler, 1st Lt. Harold E. 47
Gold Coast 11
Goldberg, Arthur J. 12, 13
Goldsberry, Pvt. Andrew E. 199
Goodman, Benny 50
Goodman, Steve 229
Gosden, Freeman 41
Gould, Chester 177, 178
Governors State University 8, 237
Graf Zeppelin 231
Graham, Billy, Center Museum 138, 139
Graham Building 192
Graham, Rev. Billy 131, 133
Grand Army of the Republic 223
Grand Army of the Republic Memorial Museum 79
Grange, Harold "Red" 13, 17, 18, 131, 133
Grant, Gen. Ulysses S. 223
Grant Park 11, 67, 68, 235, 236
Grant, Mark 218
Graue, Fred 145, 146
Graziano, Rocky 14
Great Chicago Fire of 1871 29, 30, 33, 78

243

Great Lakes Naval Training Center 122
Greater Harvard Area Historical Society 185
Greenstone Church 99
Gregg, John Robert 34
Gregg, Seaman Recruit Joseph W. 164
Gretna Station Museum/Caboose 143
Groose Point Lighthouse 109, 110
The Grove 123
The Guiding Light 41
Gullickson, Bill 218
Gumpertz, 1st Sgt. Sydney G. 47
Gunther, John 13
Gura, Larry 218
Gusenberg, Frank 60
Gusenberg, Peter 60

Haben House 113
Haeger Museum 210
Haeger Potteries 210
Hahn, Herman 236
Hagen, Jean 48
Haines House Museum 162
Haines, John C. 161, 162
Halas, George 13
Hale, Louise Closser 48
Haller, Bill 218
Haller, Tom 219
John Hancock Building 51
John Hancock Center 35
Harding Collection of Arms and Armor 81
Harding, President Warren G. 36, 135
Harkavy, Minna 235
Harney, Sp 4 Carmel B. 47
Harris, Paul P. 41
Harrison, Mayor Carter 38
Harroun, Ray 204
Hartung's License Plate and Auto Museum 123
Harvard 184
Harvard History Museum 185
Harvey, William 88
Hayes, Arthur 60
Hayes, Kathryn 217
Haymarket Riot of 1886 98
Haynes, Henry D. "Homer" 229
Heald, Capt. Nathan 21
Healy Chapel 192
Hebron 180
Hecht, Ben 49
Hedges, John 145
Hedges Station 143
Heirens, William 37, 21
Helicon Home Colony 225

Heller, Walter E., Nature Park and Interpretive Center 225
Helms, Sgt. John H. 48
Hemingway, Clarence Edmonds (Ed) 103
Hemingway, Ernest 103
Hemingway, Grace Hall 103
Hendricks, Jack 218
Henke, William D., House 126
Henry, Jacob H., House 218
Henry, John 237
Herblock 232
Here's Chicago 73
Hering, Henry 71
Hertel, Joe 94
Highland, Cpl. Patrick H. 46
Highland Park 168, 170, 234, 238
Highland Park Historical Society 169, 170
Highstein, Jene 237
Highwood 168
Hinsdale 147
Hippocrates 88
Historic Pullman Foundation 98
Historical Museum of Addision 155
Historical Society of Elmwood Park 106
Historical Society of Greater Peotone 220
Historical Society of Oak Park and River Forest 106
Hollis, Herman E. 63
Holmes, Burton 48
Holmes, Helen 48
Holmes, Henry H. 36, 37
Holmes, Stuart 48
Home Insurance Building 13
Homewood 127
Homewood Historical Museum 127
Horn, Milton 235
Horton, Pvt. William C. 48
Hostert, Bernard, Log Cabin 128
Hostert, Jacob, Log Cabin 128
Hotel Florence 98, 99
Houbolt, John C. 215, 21
Hough, Roselle A. 154
Hough House 154
Howe, Musician Orion P. 159
Hubbard, Gurdon 24
Hubble, Edwin Powell 131
Hubble's Constant 135
Hulbert, William A. 15
Hull, Charles J. 94
Hull, Cordell 226
Hull House Museum 94, 96
Humphrey, Hubert 42
Hunt, Bela 199, 200
Hunt, Richard 236, 237

Hyatt, 1st Sgt. Theodore 217
Hyde Park Art Center 237

I Will 236
IIT Research Institute 197
I & M Canal Museum 220
Ickes, Harold 42
Illini 196
Illiniwek 196
Illinois Athletic Club 14
Illinois Benedictine College 149 234
Illinois Centennial Memorial Column 236
Illinois College of Optometry 7
Illinois Institute of Technology 7, 197
Illinois Methematics and Science Academy 189
Illinois and Michigan Canal 219
Illinois and Michigan Canal National Heritage Corridor Visitors' Center 218, 219
Illinois Railway Museum 180, 182
Illinois State Museum (Lockport Gallery) 220
Illinois Youth Center—DuPage 7
Illinois Youth Center—Joliet 8
Illinois Youth Centers 8
In Celebration of the 200th Anniversary of the Founding of the Republic 236
Independence Square 236
Indians 236
Insull, Samuel 43
International Museum of Surgical Sciences and Hall of Fame 88
Iroquois Theatre Fire 38
Isle a la Cache Museum 220
Itasca 154
Itasca Historical Museum 154
Iselin, Lewis 235
Ivanhoe 171
Izzo-Pelton House 207

Jackson Park 236
Jacquard, Jerald 237
James, Jean Butz, Museum 169, 170
Jecks, Charles 177
Jenco, Rev. Lawrence Martin 215
Jenny, William L. 13
Jenter, Jack 204
Johnson, Pfc. Harold I. 47
Joliet 8, 213, 214, 215, 217, 218, 219, 220
Joliet Area Historical Society and Museum 218
Joliet Army Ammunition Plant 213

Joliet Correctional Center 8, 213, 215
Joliet, Louis 21
Joliet Motor Co. 216
Joliet Municipal Airport Hangar 218
Joliet Township High School 218
Jones, Robert 236
Jordan, Jim 41
Jordan, Marian 41
Josef, Franz, land 229
Joyce, James 50
Judson College 8
Jurica Natural History Museum 149, 234
Jurica, Rev. Hilary S. 149

KYW 41
Kane County 7, 189
Kane, Senator Elias K. 8
Kaufmann, John S. 126
Keller, Sgt. Leonard B. 47
Kelly, Edward J. 43
Kelly, Ellsworth 236
Kelly, Pvt. John J. 47
Kemeys, Edward 235, 236
Kenilworth 111
Kenilworth Historical Museum 111
Kennedy, President John F. 228
Kennicott House 123
Kent, Trumball 119
Keystone Building 192
Ketsinger, Pvt. George 46
Keystone Studios 233
Kolmon, Alvin, Jr. 215
Kincaid House 121
"King of the Bombers" 58
Kinzie, John 21, 24
Kohlsaat, Herman H. 37
Kondrake, Morton 217
Koniuszy, Bronislaw 236
Kosciusko, Thaddeus 94
Krotiak, Pfc. Anthony L. 47
Krupa, Gene 50
Kruse House Museum 145
Kryzowski, Capt. Edward C. 47
Kubelsky, Benjamin 159

LaGrange 123
LaGrange Historical Museum 123
Ladd Arboretum and Ecology Center 109
Lady Elgin 29
Lager Beer Riots 26
Lake Bluff 168
Lake County 8, 159, 171, 172
Lake County Forest Preserve 173

245

Lake County Museum 172, 173
Lake Forest 166, 237 238
Lake Forest College 8
Lakeland 182, 185
Lalime, Jean 21
Landis, Jessie Royce 48
Landis, Kenesaw Mountain 227
Landmark Museum of the Bremen Historical Society of Tinley Park 127
Lane, John, Sr. 219
Lang, Lois Delander 215
Langum Park 195, 202
Lansing 127
Lansing Historical Museum 127
Lardner, Ring 50
Large Two Forms 237
Larkin Office Building 103
LaRocque, Rod 48
LaSalle, 219
LaSalle Hotel Fire 46
LaSalle, Sieur de 21
Lawrence, D. H. 50
Lawrence of Arabia 183
Leiber, Fritz 48
Leims, 2nd Lt. John H. 48
Leonard, Robert Z. 48
Leopold, Nathan F., Jr. 37, 213
LeRoy Oakes Forest Preserve 201, 202
Lewis, Herbert R. 22
Lewis University 8
Libertyville 170, 171
Libertyville-Mundelein Historical Society 171, 172
Lilacia Park 143
Lincoln, Abraham 26, 29, 126, 159, 210
Lincoln, Abraham statue 235
Lincoln, Mary Todd 194, 195
Lincoln Park 11, 88, 235, 236
Lindbergh, Charles 46
Lions 236
Lindsay, Vachel 50
Lingg, Louis 34
Lingle, Jake 55, 56
Lisle 146, 234
Lisle Depot Museum 150
Little Fort 159
Little Fort Porcupine and Democratic Banner 159
Little Fort Trading Post 159
Little Home Church 156
Little Red Schoolhouse Nature Center 234
Living Bible 134
Livingston, Al 204

Lizzardo Museum of Lapidary Art 141
Lockport 219
Loeb and Leopold 13
Loeb, Richard A. 37, 213
Logan, John Alexander 223
Loman, Pvt. Berger 47
Lombard 143
Lombardo, Antonio 56
Long, Richard 48
Longman, Evelyn Beatrice 236
Loop 11
Lord, Jimmy 50
Lord, Mr. & Mrs. G. P. 207
Louis, Joe 14
Lovell General Hosptial No. 28 168
Loyola University 237
Loyola University of Chicago 7
Loyola University Medical Center 237
Lusic, Lt. Carl 217
Lynch, Sgt. Allen J. 47

Madarik, Elmer "Tippy" 218
Magnificent Mile 11, 22
Maher, George W. 106
Mallinckrodt College of the North Shore 7
Marengo 183
Marquette, Father Jacques 21
Marsala, Joseph Francis "Joe" 50
Marseilles 219
Marshall Field & Company 31
Martin D'Arcy Gallery of Art 237
Marx, Gustav 38
Mary and Leigh Block Gallery 237
Master, Edgar Lee 50
Mattiasson, Kurt 94
May, John 60
Maywood 237
McCambridge, Mercedes 217
McCartan, Edward 235
McCarthy, Capt. Joseph J. 48
McCarthy, Charlie 48
McClure's Magazine 225
McCormick, Cyrus H. 26, 31
McCormick, Robert R. 13, 131, 133, 135, 136
McCormick Robert R., Museum 135, 138
McCullough, Geraldine 236
McDonald, Jessica North 147
McGrath, Paul 48
McGraw, Sgt. Thomas 46
McGurn, Jack "Machine Gun" 60
McHenry 8, 177, 184
McHenry, Col. William 177
McHenry County 8, 177, 184

McHenry County Historical Society Museum 179, 180
McHenry, Gen. William 8
McSwiggin, Assistant States Attorney William 55
Medical Center 7
Medill, Joseph 24, 135
Memorial Day 223
Memorial Bridge 191
Merchandise Mart 11
Merchandise Mart Hall of Fame 235
Merchants Club of Chicago 164
Merkle Cabin Historical Museum 120
Mestrovic, Ivan 236
Mexican Fine Arts Center Museum 92
Meyers, Nicholas 113
Michael, 1st Lt. Edward S. 47
Midway Airport 46
Midwest Stock Exchange 11
Mies van der Rohe, Ludwig 13
Mike the Devil 57
Millay, Edna St. Vincent 50
Milnes, Sherrill 131, 147, 148
Milton, Tommy 204
Mikan, George 218
Miro, Joan 235
Miro's Chicago 235
Miss, Mary 237
Mitchell, Betty 109
Mitchell, John 109
Mitchell, Everett 131, 134
Mitchell, Indian Museum 109
Mohlman, Ted 145
Monroe, Harriet 50
Monroe, Pfc. James H. 189
Monster of Sixty Third Street 36
Montgomery Wards 31
Monument to Johann Wolfgang Van Goethe 236
Monument with Standing Beast 235
Moody Bible Institute 34
Moody, Dwight L. 26, 34
Moody Memorial Church 34
Moody Press 34
Moore, Henry 236, 237
Moran, George "Bugs" 55, 56, 58, 60
Moran, Lee 48
Moran, Polly 48
Morning News 232
Morr, "Skip" 50
Morris 219
Morrison, William 37
Morton Arboretum 149
Morton Grove 113
Morton Grove Historical Museum 113
Morton, J. Sterling 149

Morton, Joy 149
Moskala, Pfc. Edward J. 47
Mother Theresa Museum 127
Motley, Willard, 49
Mount Prospect 115
Mount Prospect Historical Museum 115, 118
Mudgett, Dr. Herman W. 36, 37
Muir, Gavin 48
Mulford, Ralph 204
Muller House 114
Mulligan, Charles J. 236
Mullin, Seaman Hugh P. 180
Mundelein 170, 171, 172
Mundelein College 7
Mundelein, George Cardinal 172
Muntz, Earl "Madman" 204, 205, 206
Muntz Jet 206
Murphy, Ed 218
Museum of Broadcast Communications 96
Museum of Contemporary Art 88, 89, 90
Museum of Contemporary Photography 79
Museum of Holography 95, 96
Museum of Science and Industry 82, 83, 84

National Basketball Association 11, 15
National College of Education 8
National Football League 11, 15
National Heritage Corridor 219
National Hockey League 11, 15
National League 11
Naper, Capt. Joseph 131, 149
Naper Settlement 149, 150, 151
Naperville 149, 150, 151
Nathan Manilow Sculpture Park 237
Naval Air Reserve Training Command Headquarters 123
Naval Training Center, Great Lakes 163, 164
Naval Training Station 168
Neal, Tom 107
Near Eastside Historic District 192
Near Northwest Historic District 192
Neebe, Oscar E. 34
Nelson, George "Baby Face" 55, 63
Nesbit, Miriam 48
Ness, Eliott 57, 58
Nettleton, Lois 177
Nevelson, Louise 235
Newberry, Lane K. 147
Newman, Paul 177

Nicholas Copernicus 236
Niedemeyer, Peter 38
Niles 113
Niles Center 63, 113
Niles Historical Museum 114
1937 Memorial Day Massacre 43
1926 Battles of the Standard Oil Building 57
Nitti, Frank 60
Nobel Prize 49
Noel's Livery Barn 216
Norge N. 231
Noguchi, Isamu 236
Norkiewicz, Joseph 215
Norris, Dellora Angell 199
North Central College 151, 164
North Park College 7
North Park Village Nature Center 234
North Shore Art League 237
North Side 11, 56
North, Sterling 147
Northbrook 234
Northeastern Illinois University 7
Northern Baptist Theological Seminary 7
Northern Land 229
Northwestern University 8, 36, 119, 229
Novak, Robert 217
Nuclear Energy 236

Oak Brook 145, 146, 234
Oak Park 103, 104, 106, 107
Oak Park Conservatory 106
Oaklawn Residence 156
Oak Woods Cemetery 27, 28
Oakwood Cemetery, Joliet 218
O'Banion, Charles Dion "Deanie" 56, 57, 60
Sister Guala O'Connor Art Gallery 238
O'Connor, Thomas "Terrible Tommy" 37
Octagon House 119, 121
Offerman, George, Jr. 49
O'Hara, John 50
O'Hare, Lt. Edward "Butch" 45, 46, 228
Old Courthouse and Jail 177
Old Graue Mill and Museum 145, 146, 147
"Old Main" 205, 207
Old Town 11
Oldenberg, Claes 235
Oldfield, Barney 204
O'Leary's, Mrs. Patrick, cow 29
Olive, Pfc. Milton L. 47

Olmstead, Gertrude 49
Olmsted, Frederick Law 107
1,000 Mile Horse Race, The 37
O'Neill, Lottie Holman 147, 223
O'Neill, Patrick J. 37
Orchard Field 228
Orchard, Frank 50
Oriental Institute 90, 91
Orland Park 128
Osborne, Lt. (jg) Weedon E. 48
Ostend 177
Ottawa 219
Ouilmette, Antoine 24, 111
Our Lady of Angels School 46
Ovaltine Company 143
Owens Home 184

Paarlberg Farmstead Homestead 126
Paderewski, Ignace 94
Page, Geraldine 177
Pajeau, Charles 107
Palace Car Company 98
Palatine 115
Palatine Historical Society 115
Palmer, Betsy 177
Palmer, Col. Gustavius 183, 184, 186
Palmer, Henriette 183, 184, 186
Palmer House 26, 183
Palmer, Potter 26, 224
Palmolive Building 22
Paramount Arts Center 191
Park Forest 238
Park Forest Art Center 238
Parker, Jill 236
Parks, Larry 217
Parsons, Alberta R. 34
Pasteur, Louis 88
Patton, 2nd Lt. George S., Jr. 165, 170
Payne, John 237
Payne, Capt. Morgan 149
Paxton, Cynthia 151
Paxton, Thompson 151
Payton, Walter 15, 16
Peace Museum 98
Pearson, Drew 107
Peart, Jerry 237
Peers, Joan 49
Peotone 220
Perciali, Michael 109
Perciali, Rodica 109
Percival, Walter C. 49
Perconte, Jack 218
Perry, Judge Joseph Sam 138, 143
The Perry Mastodon 138, 139
Pershing, Gen. John "Black Jack" 168
Personnel Support Activity 168

Perez, Pfc. Manuel 47
Periolat, George 49
Picasso, Pablo 39, 235, 237
Pietzel, Benjamin F. 37
"Pineapple Primary" 58
Pinkerton, Allan 207, 209, 210
Pioneer Settlement 220
Pioneer Sleeping Car 34
Pioneer Sholes School 201, 202
Pittsfield Building 31
Plainfield 218
Plainfield Historical Society Museum 219
Plainfield House 219
Pleasant Home 106
Poetry 50
Polasek, Albin 236
Polish Museum of America 87, 92, 94
Pollack, Ben 50
Pony Inn 55
Porter, Rev. Jeremiah 24
Pottawatomi Indians 198, 199
Pope, Cpl. Thomas A. 194
Powell, John Wesley 131
Power, Paul 49
Powers, Cp. Wesley J. 204
Powers, John A. "Shorty" 147
"Prairie Avenue Set" 224
Prairie House 86
Prehistoric Life Museum 109
Prendergast, Patrick E. 38
Price, Ramon Bertell 236
Printers Row Printing Museum 96
Pro Football Hall of Fame 13, 18
Prohibition 55, 56
Proctor, Alexander Phimister 236
Pulitzer Prize 49
Pullman 34, 99, 100
Pullman, George M. 34, 98, 99, 222
Pullman Palace Car Company 34
Pullman Strike of 1894 98, 126
Purvis, Melvin 60
Puryear, Martin 237

Quereau House 194

Raupp Memorial Museum 114
H. A. Rathje Dutch Mill 220
Reber, Grote 131, 134
Rebissdo, Louis T. 236
Reicher Gallery 238
Record 232
Recruit Training Command 164, 165
Red Oak Farm 135
Reed, Jeff 218

Regensteiner Publishing Enterprises, Inc. 172
Regional Transportation Center 191
Renaissance Society 238
Republic Steel Corporation 43
Rentner, Ernst "Pug" 218
The Republic 236
Reserve Training Command 123
Rialto Square Theater 218
Ricca, Paul "The Waiter" 60
Rice, Grantland 17
Richardson, Henry Hobson 92, 224
Richie, Lionel 217
Richman, Charles 49
Richmond 180, 184
Rickenbacker, Eddie 204
Ridgely, John 49
River Forest 234, 238
River Grove 106
River Trail Nature Center 234
Riverbank Laboratories 197
Riverside 107
Riverside Historical Museum 107
Robbins, Gale 49
Robie, Frederick C. 84
Robie House 84, 86, 103
Roche, James M. 204, 205
Rodin, Gil 50
Roebuck, Alvah C. 31
Roentgen, Wilhelm 88
Roeski, Emil 38
Rolling Meadows 237
Rosary College 238
Romanian Folk Art Museum 109
Romeoville 220
Roosevelt, Franklin D. 42
Roosevelt, President Theodore 164
Roosevelt University 7
Roselle 154
Rosemont 119
Rosary College 7
Rosenbaum, Paul and Gabrilla 81
Rosenwald, Julius 84
Ross, Barney 14
Rotary Club 41
Rovelstad, Trygve A. 203
Rox, Henry 235
Russell, Gail 49
Ryan, Robert 48
Ryerson, Edward L., Conservation Area 234

S.M.C. Cartage Company 60
St. Charles 151, 189, 195, 197, 198, 199, 200, 201, 204

St. Charles Historical Society Museum 200, 202
St. Charles (IL) School for Boys 63
Saint-Gaudens, Augustus 235, 236
St. Mary of the Lake Seminary 172
St. Valentine's Day massacre 60
St. Xavier College 7
Sage, Anna 60
Sand Ridge Nature Center 234
Sandburg, Carl 49, 50
Sangerman, Joseph 58
Saylor, Syd 49
Scalise, John 57
Schaumburg 119, 120, 122
Schmitt, Harrison (astronaut) 105
School of Holography 96
Schroeder, Sgt. Henry F. 46
Schuette, Henry 115
Schwab, Michael 34
Scopes, John T. 13, 226
Scripps, John T. 24
Sears, Joseph 111
Sears, Richard W. 31
Sears Roebuck and Company 31, 73, 84
Sears Tower 35, 51
Sebille, Major Louis J. 47
Seidel, Emory 191
Service School Command 168
Seven Acres Antique Village and Museum 178, 180, 181
Shedd, John Graves 67
Shedd, John G., Aquarium 67, 69, 70
Sheppard, Robert D. 107
Sheridan, Gen. Philip H. 166, 168
Sherman, Gen. William T. 233
"silk stocking" ward 218
Sills, Milton 49
Simpson, Cassino Wendell 50
Sinclair, Upton 235
6th Infantry 168
Skinner, Cornelia Otis 49
Skokie 113
Skokie Historical Society 113
Smart, David and Alfred, Gallery 238
Smith, George W., house 106
Snerd, Mortimer 48
Socialist Labor Party 31
Softball 227
Soldier Field 11, 14
Sonnenschein Gallery 238
Sounding Sculpture 235
Sousa, Lt. Cmdr. John Philip 164
South Elgin 189, 207, 208
South Holland 126, 234
South Holland Museum 126

South Side 11, 34, 41, 43, 44, 230
South Side Community Art Center 238
Speck, Richard 213
Spertus College of Judaica 7, 81
Spertus Museum of Judaica 80, 81
Spies, August 31, 34
Spiezio, Eddie 218
Spirit of DuSable Sculpture Garden, The 236
Spring Valley Nature Sanctuary 120
Sri Vendateswara Swami Temple of Greater Chicago 194
Stacy, Moses 143
Stacy's Tavern 143, 144
Stagg, Amos Alonzo 14
Standard Oil Building 51
Stanley Cup 15
Stanwyck, Barbara 122
Starr, Ellen Gates 94
Stateville Prison 8, 213, 214, 215
State of Illinosi Art Gallery 238
Statuary Hall 36
Stedman, Myrtle 49
Steele, Albert B. 172
Steers, Larry 49
Stephens, Donald E. Museum of Hummel and European Folk Art 119
Stettinius, Edward R. 226
Stolp Island 192
Stolp Island Historic District 192
Stolp, Joseph 192
Stolp Woolen Mill Store 192
Stone, John 26
Stone, Melvin J. 232
Stone, Ormond 232
Storrs, John 235
Strautmanis, Edvins 237
Stupey, Francis, log cabin 170
Suburban Fine Art Center 238
Sullivan, Louis Henri 13, 234, 235
Sumner, Pvt. James 46
Sudakis, Bill 218
Sundial 236
Susquehanna (PA) University 14
Swanson, Gloria 40, 49, 233
Swedish American Historical Society 94
Swedish American Museum 94
Sweeney, Jim 58
Sweet, Blanche 48

Taft, Lorado 203, 231, 235, 236
Taylor, Dr. Kenneth 131, 134
Taylor, Lawrence E. 236
Taylor, Robert 122

Teale, Edwin Way 217
Teich, Curt 172
Telephony Museum 96
Terra, Daniel J. 73
Terra Museum of American Art 72, 73
Terrible Gennas 57
Texaco Oil Company 131, 133, 199
Thaddeus Kosciuszko Memorial 236
Thayer, Tom 218
Thomas Garrigue Masaryk Memorial 236
Thompson Burying Grounds 177
Thompson Inn 177
Thompson, William Hale "Big Bill" 58, 230
Thompson, Mrs. Lucretia 26
Thorne, George R. 31
Thorne, Mrs. James Ward 81
Thorvaldsen, Bertel 236
Times-Herald 235
Tinley Park 127
Tinkertoys 107
Tonti, Henry 21
Tony the Gentleman 57
Totter, Audrey 217
Torrio, John 55
Touhy, Roger "The Terrible" 63, 213
Town of Little Fort 159
Tracy, Dick 177, 178
Trailside Museum of Natural History 234
Treaty of Prairie du Chien 111
Tribune Tower 32, 79
Trinity College 8
Triton College 105, 106, 107
Truemper, 2nd Lt. Walter E. 189
Tucker automobile 43, 44
Tucker, Preston 43, 44
Tunney, Gene 14
Turpin, Ben 49

U.S.S. Bennington 47
U.S.S. Chicago 48
U.S.S. Fletcher 180
U.S.S. Lexington 46
U.S.S. Wheaton 135
Ukrainian National Museum 93, 94
Ulysses S. Grant Memorial 236
Umlauf, Charles 235
Union 179, 180, 181, 182
Union Station 218
Union Stock Yards 13, 24, 43, 154
United States Steel 131, 134
Unity Temple 103, 106
University of Chicago 14, 37, 43, 57, 90, 91, 131, 230, 236, 238

University of Illinois 7
University of Illinois Circle Campus 237
University Park 237
Untitled Light Sculpture 236
"The Untouchables" 57, 58
Upton, Robert "Bob" 217

Valli, Virginia 49
Van Alstyne, Egbert Anson 183
Van Buren, Mabel 49
Van Buren, President Martin 213
van Dine, Harvey 38
Van Harvey, Art 41
Van Horne, Sir William 218
Van Oostenbrugge Centennial Home 126
Vandercook College of Music 7
Vaux, Calvert 107
Venuti, Joe 229
Vernon, Bobby 49
Vernon Hills 170, 172
Vesota, Bruno 49
Victory, World War I Black Soldiers' Memorial 237
Vietnam Museum 94
Villa Park 141
Villa Park Historical Society Museum 141
Virgil 204
Vita 237
Vivyan, John 48
Voliva, Wilber Glenn 162
Volk, Leonard Wells 29, 236
Volo 174
Volo Antique Auto Museum and Village 174

WFLD-TV, (Channel 32) 31
Wadhams/Young House 126
Walker, Nella 49
Wanamacher/Menke archaeological site 127
Ward, A. Montgomery 31
Warden, Cpl. John 46
Warren, C. Denier 49
Warren, Col. Julius M. 152
Warrenville 152
Warrenville Historical Society 152, 153
Washburn, Bryant 49
Washburn, Lt. G. A. T. 122
Washington Birthday Massacre 215
Washington Park 236
Washington Post 232
Water Tower Pumping Station 33, 73, 78, 85

251

Wauconda 172, 173, 174
Wauconda Township Historical Society 172
Waukegan 8, 159, 160, 161
Waukegan Historical Society 159, 160
Wayne 154, 156
Weber, L/Cpl. Lester W. 189
Weinberg, Arthur 226
Weinman, Adolph Alexander 235
Weinshank, Al 60
Weiss, Hymie 56, 57
Weiss, Morton B., Museum of Judaica, K.A.M. 96
Weissmuller, Johnny 14
Welles, Orson 177
West Chicago 145
West Chicago Historical Museum 145
West Dundee 189, 207, 209
West Side 11, 41, 226
Western Springs 123
Western Springs Historical Society Museum 123, 124
Weston, Henry 177
Westside Historic District 192
Wheaton, 132, 133, 135, 140
Wheaton College 7, 138, 139, 143
Wheaton Historic Preservation Council 141
"The Wheaton Iceman" 17
Wheeling 114
Wheeling Historical Museum 115
Whistler, Capt. John 21
White, Capt. Patrick H. 46
White Sox 14
Whitman, Gayne 48
Wigwam 26
Will, Conrad 8
Will County 8, 213
Will County Historical Society 219

Willard, Francis Elizabeth Caroline 36, 107
Williams, Horrace 119
Willow Springs 234
Willowbrook Forest Preserve 142
Willowbrook Wildlife Haven 143, 234
Wilmette 111, 112
Wilmette Historical Museum 111
Wilmington 220
Wilmington Area Historical Society 220
Winfield 143
Winnetka 63, 113, 237
Winnetka Historical Museum 113
Wishart, Spencer 204
Wittenmyer, Annie 36
Women's Christian Temperance Union (WCTU) 36, 107
Wood Dale 154
Wood Dale Historical Society 154
Woodstock 8, 177, 178, 180, 183, 184
Woodstock Opera House 177
World's Columbian Exposition 38
Wright, Frank Lloyd 13, 84, 86, 103, 106, 196, 197, 234
Wright, Frank Lloyd, home and studio 103, 104
Wrigley Field 11, 17
Wynekoop, Dr. Alice Lindsay 37

Young, Capt. Gerald O. 47

Zale, Tony 14
Zangara, Guiseppe 42
Zimmerman, A. L. "Al" 215, 217
Zinn, Walter 43
Zion 162
Zion Historical Society 164
Zouaves 29